The Gospel Ac

the Briae

"Stay dressed for action and
keep your lamps burning"
Luke 12:35 [ESV]

"If I find in myself desires which nothing in this world can satisfy, the only logical explanation is that I was made for another world."

— Mere Christianity by CS Lewis

The Gospel According to the Bride (Volume 1)

Preparing the warrior bride

for the days ahead

Mike Pike
Call2Come

Dedication

I dedicate this work to my glorious Saviour and Bridegroom King the Lord Jesus Christ who has touched my life in more ways than I could ever number. I present this as my offering to Him in the hope and prayer others might find extra oil to keep their lamps in their vigil awaiting the Day when He returns for His Bride.

Recommendation

Mike is not just the co-director with me of the Call2Come movement but is a very dear friend too. From the moment we first met in 2007 at an intercessors' meeting in our home county Cornwall, England, we knew this was one of God's 'Divine appointments'. I have been privileged to journey with him ever since on our path of discovery about the Bride, and in our response to the Spirit's invitation to 'come up a little higher' in pursuit of our Bridegroom King. This has taken us to many nations around the world as together we have sought to awaken and prepare the Bride in these end times. It has been such a joy to share a conference platform with him, engaging in prophetic ministry to declare a prophetic word over a nation or share in some prophetic action in obedience to the Spirit of God.

Whatever Mike does is done so with such great integrity and humility, with an awareness of the seriousness of the responsibility laid upon us, and the awesomeness of the mandate under which we serve. When it comes to his writing, he labours with the same degree of sensitivity and desire for correctness. Every sentence he writes is carefully crafted and every word is laboured over as a seed being sown which must bear precious fruit. As a result, nothing is either over or understated. He has a great gift of writing. Coupled with his keen mind to unravel the minutiae of a subject and bring all those threads together against the backdrop of the bigger picture, enables him firstly, to understand complex subjects, but then also present them to us in a clear and precise logical sequence. It is only someone with this sort of gifting that could write such a challenging and unique subject as '*The Gospel according to the Bride*'. As Mike often says, "When you have seen the Bride and Bridegroom as the central themes in the Scriptures, you can never be the same again or unsee".

Such a revelation changes your whole perception. Everything is then seen through the lens of the Bride and subsequently opens you up to new avenues of revelation and depths of intimacy with the Lord. If the word gospel means 'Good News', then this book is certainly good news. This is the Good News about the Bride. My prayer is that in reading it you will be drawn deeper into intimacy with Jesus but also through the lens of the Bride you will begin to make more sense of some other difficult theological and eschatological issues.

Howard Barnes
Co-Director, Call2Come International

Contents

Introduction

It was Valentine's Day 2008 when the Lord dramatically touched my heart and commissioned me to 'Romance His Bride'. It followed a time in my life that many who have experienced it call 'The Dark Night of the Soul'. It was for me a season of eight wilderness years, feeling rejected, alone and in despair; surrounded by palpable darkness and a dogged depression I had known all my life up to that time. Yet despite all the pain of those years, there remained in me a single flame; a candle that had not yet gone out but still burnt with a deep love for God. Leading up to Valentine's Day I had a growing sense of the Lord wanting to speak to me, and I knew to hear from Him I would need to position myself before Him in a way that would allow an uninterrupted and extended time of being still so I could just simply kneel and listen for as long as it would take.

I didn't know where my spiritual journey would take me back then, but I shared with my wife Jo how the Lord was calling me into a time alone with Him. Being the wonderful woman and support she has always been, Jo sent me with her blessing to go and hear from the Lord. I travelled 400 kilometres to an isolated location and booked a hotel room for three days armed only with my Bible and some worship music. After checking in and closing the hotel room door behind me, I put on the worship music and knelt beside the bed with a feeling of excitement and expectancy. Now, I don't know about you, but for me, this was a very difficult thing to do. The moment we try to be still, we become conscious of so many thoughts like traffic passing through our minds, pleading for our attention.

Creating noise and disruption, they become a direct barrier to the sacred discipline of meditation. This is how it was for me, but as I knelt beside the bed, despite the barrage of distractions buzzing through my head, I determined not to move until I knew I had heard from the Lord.

After an hour I turned down the music so now it just played quietly, I pressed in deeper. Another hour and the music was faded again, then another passed until an absolute silence pervaded outside but more importantly, within me. In that stillness, I was aware of the tangible presence of God. A very holy place like no other; a place beyond description yet incredibly real. For three days I was alone with Him, learning to listen, and during that time He spoke and showed me visions. But the things I saw disturbed me greatly. My spirit was troubled and broken, sensing a glimpse of what He saw and felt. In one vision, I saw the church distracted by many things and seduced by the pleasures of this world. The Lord was not among her but outside watching. Those three days changed my life and set me on a new course to 'Romance the Bride' and call her back to intimacy with Him as her Bridegroom.

Arriving home, I was excited to share with Jo all the Lord had revealed and commissioned us to. We cleared a room in our Cornish cottage and dedicated it as holy unto the Lord; it was a sanctuary within our home, a place for listening to His heart. In fact, I couldn't even enter the room until after I had prayed! Before I had permission to enter, I would have a time of prayer outside, until I sensed the peace and invitation to go deeper. And that's how it was back then and ever since I have maintained the discipline of meditation and being still in His presence. It has always been in these times of solitude, alone with the Lord, where I have heard the gentle whispers of His love for me and for His Bride. It was there in the cleft of the rock I witnessed His glory and received the wisdom and vision for Call2Come. It has been the place He continually draws me to and grants insight for the prophetic mantle I have accepted. This is not spoken prayer but the listening of a heart intent on a deeper truth and experience. For there is a place deeper than words can take us: beyond the limitation of human language into a realm defined by His heart and His Word. Today, His Spirit is leading us there to encounter Him more than ever before.

The Lord is calling us to come away with Him to a place reserved only for Him and His Bride. It is a strange and unfamiliar land; uncharted territory with unseen horizons stretching far. I do not speak of an imaginary place but one which is more real than the physical world we have grown accustomed to. For there has come an increased superimposition of the unseen realm breaking into our familiarity and redefining what we once thought we knew and understood. The Bride occupies this convergence between the spiritual and physical spheres, she is uniquely commissioned and empowered as a royal emissary to give assent to decrees legislated in Heaven's throne room and to transact them upon the earth. There are prayers only she can pray, songs only she can sing, authority only she can wield and assignments that only she can fulfil. The rhythm of church life we have known for so long has changed and continues to change. The old must give way to the new, yet in truth, this 'new' paradigm resonates with an ancient anointing that we have simply forgotten. We have gazed at our reflection in stagnant waters for too long and forgotten who we are. But the Holy Spirit has stirred those waters and muddled perceptions, enabling us to reimagine our primeval identity. But take note, this is not a licence to redefine our roots rather awaken that which is latent and quicken that long since woven into our core DNA.

If the Bride is to get dressed, she must first awake, by this I mean she must ascend into a new consciousness. The dictionary defines consciousness as the state of being aware of and responsive to one's surroundings, and a person's perception of something. When someone in a coma gains consciousness, we might say they have woken up. This is how it is for the Bride. But bridal awakening goes beyond awareness or perception and enters into a new consciousness. It is an ascension into the mind of Christ and is prophetic. This mind enables her to see in both realities: that which is seen and that which is unseen. Having the mind of Christ empowers her to see in both worlds. Living with this bridal consciousness requires living from a place of intimacy and abiding in the Bridegroom so that her perspective and vision is changed because she is looking through a different lens, a different mindset, a different heart.

If the Bride is to prepare for the days ahead, then she must have a reliable roadmap upon which she can navigate the terrain before her and discern the significance of world events as they unfold. This is my objective for this first volume of The Gospel According to the Bride; To look again at scripture from. a Bridal perspective. It is a compilation of sixty short podcasts I released during the lockdown months of 2020 and 2021 that I called Quick Bites, in which I systematically begin to look at scripture and in particular eschatology from a bridal perspective. This volume starts with shorter Bites easier to digest; laying a foundation precept upon precept, of who the Bride is, bringing her to life and giving her a voice. Then as we progress, the subjects will become more in-depth and difficult, so I encourage you to take your time and even use this volume as a two-month devotional (which is what I originally had in mind). To assist your study, I have added 200 footnotes and scripture references to expand upon some points I had made in the original podcasts. Inevitably, there may be things you see differently and that's okay, only let not differences lead to division. My intention is not to offend or disregard your position on matters of the end times, but to provide a solid biblical rationale and blueprint to equip the Bride for the days ahead. It is my firm conviction the Bride is mandated, like John the Baptist in the spirit of Elijah, to prepare the way of the Lord and will therefore remain upon the earth all the way up to the Day of the Lord. I'm so excited you have a copy of this work in your hands, my prayer is that you will be greatly encouraged and inspired in your own journey towards the Bridegroom. Let's begin!

My beloved spoke, and said to me: "Rise up, my love, my fair one, and come away. For lo, the winter is past, the rain is over and gone. The flowers appear on the earth; The time of singing has come, and the voice of the turtledove is heard in our land. The fig tree puts forth her green figs, and the vines with the tender grapes give a good smell. Rise up, my love, my fair one, and come away! O my dove, in the clefts of the rock, In the secret places of the cliff, let me see your face, let me hear your voice; For your voice is sweet, and your face is lovely." (Song Of Songs 2:10-14)

QB1 Who is the Bride?

T he Bride comes out of the Bridegroom because she has to be of the same DNA as Him to be compatible with Him. Only that which is from the Bridegroom can be joined back to Him[1]. The Bride is the one who will be joined together with the Lord in the harmony of a marriage union when He returns to reign upon the Earth[2]. She is neither Jew nor Gentile but a corporate new creation and spiritual being. Though her roots can be seen in natural Israel, she transcends natural Israel because her origin was before and her destiny to reign with Jesus will be after. She has always been in the heart of God, and the Father purposed that He would give the Bride as a love gift to the Son.

We are about to embark on a voyage through scripture in our quest to discover, identify, understand and answer this question: Who is the Bride? I encourage you to take your time and see this as a journey of intimacy towards the Bridegroom. The Holy Spirit will help you along each step of the way, all you need to begin is a willingness to go where He leads. Our voyage will cross some turbulent seas, spanning depths we may never have encountered before. For sure, we will need an open mind and teachable heart, we will need tenacity

---

[1] We find this principle at the very beginning in the Creation narrative. Before sin ever entered the world, we are given the foreshadow of Jesus and His Bride through Adam and Eve. Just as the only suitable partner for Adam came from out of Adam, so also with the Bride of Jesus Christ.
[2] This is the very first prophecy in scripture. Therefore a man shall leave his father and mother and be joined to his wife, and they shall become one flesh. (Genesis 2:24).

and a passion for the Word. Some will find the journey too great a diversion from their current course and turn back to more familiar waters, while others will find their hearts so stirred and resonating within them that they cross over a threshold they will never return to. My prayer is you will stay the course and that I have provided sufficient scriptural support and sound biblical exegesis to undergird the things shared. Let's begin with a prayer:

Heavenly Father, thank you for all that you have done for me. Thank you for drawing me near into a loving relationship with you as your child which I cherish so dearly. Thank you for the gift of your Son Jesus, who has become not only my Saviour, but my Bridegroom also. Help me Holy Spirit to understand these glories more fully as I welcome you once more into my life today. Fill me afresh, quicken me and open the eyes of my heart that I may see more clearly the fullness of all that awaits me, and especially what it means to be included as part of the Bride. Lead me to the Bridegroom that I may lay at His feet and there give my heart once more in adoration and desire. Jesus, I come to you, lost in wonder, love and praise. Not knowing how I might approach, except your love beckons me near.

Amen.

QB2 Is the Church the Bride?

This depends upon what we mean when we say church. The word church is the word *'ekklesia'* and means a called-out assembly. The word *'ekklesia'* is not unique to Christianity or even to the New Testament. In Acts 7:38 it reads:

This is he who was in the congregation in the wilderness with the Angel who spoke to him on Mount Sinai, and with our fathers, the one who received the living oracles to give to us.

This verse in Acts speaks of Moses leading the congregation (or assembly), which is the word *'ekklesia'*, (or church). The concept of church is common to both the Old and New Testaments. Note that Moses led the called-out assembly from Egypt to Sinai which is the place where Israel became consummated as a nation and also betrothed to Jehovah in marriage. Being the *'ekklesia'* is a transitory state that leads to marriage. As the church, we are the called-out assembly and like Moses led Israel out of Egypt, through the Red Sea and the Wilderness to Mount Sinai, so also Jesus leads out His *'ekklesia'* from captivity to betrothal. Being the church is the beginning of our journey, being the Bride is our destiny. So, to answer our question: is the church the Bride? We will always be the called-out assembly and therefore we will always be His church, but we must also understand that we are a called-out assembly (i.e., the church) to be the Bride. [3]

> *The church cannot remain where she is, she must go beyond the threshold of the church into the destiny of being the Bride. She must go deeper and not only relate to Jesus as the Saviour but also as her Bridegroom.* [4]

If we do not allow the Holy Spirit to take us on that journey, then we may find though we are the church, we may never be ready as the Bride.

---

[3] Ephesians 5:22-33 In this well-known passage on husbands and wives, Paul begins by exhorting husbands to love their wives as Christ loved the church, but then he reverses the flow of emphasis and reveals how our understanding of husband and wife should be applied to Christ and the church. Paul quotes from Genesis 2:24, how a man will leave his father and mother and be joined to his wife so that they become 'one flesh' and ascribes this to Jesus and the church as His Bride.

[4] John the Baptist went on this same journey of revelation about Jesus Christ. In John 1:29 he testifies to Jesus as 'the Lamb of God who takes away the sin of the world,' then in John 3:29 John's witness has moved beyond Jesus as Saviour to Jesus as the Bridegroom. Interestingly, separating these two accounts is the wedding at Cana in John 2. For more information on this journey and transition refer to my eBook 'The Bride in the Wilderness'

QB3 Are the Ten Virgins in Matthew 25 the Bride?

In the parable of the ten virgins in Matthew 25:1-13, the Bridegroom was delayed in coming and therefore the oil the virgins started with was not enough to last the duration of the night. Jesus used this parable to teach on the importance of our individual preparation for the Bridegroom's coming, and in particular, we should have extra oil, so our lamps do not run out before He returns. Now because there is only one Bride[5], and Jesus is addressing our individual responsibility to be ready, the characters He used to teach this principle are ten virgins and not one Bride. This way the difference between wisdom and foolishness can be illustrated on a personal level. Individually, none of the virgins were the Bride, but the five wise virgins corporately together were. Because the Bride doesn't feature explicitly in this parable[6], some argue the virgins are therefore not the Bride but remember Paul used

---

[5] The concept of one Bride is not universally accepted across the church, and much confusion and range of opinion currently exist. In particular, the largest factor determining this divide comes from the dispensational position which segregates Israel and the Church. We shall examine this position thoroughly later.

[6] In scripture, Jesus never referred directly to His Bride but chose rather to teach about His wedding through parables. In each of these parables the Bride is never mentioned. Obviously, this does not negate the existence of His Bride, but what it does do is keep her veiled, and focus the spotlight on personal preparation and devotion.

the term virgin clearly referring to the Bride in 2 Corinthians 11:2 where he writes:

For I am jealous for you with a godly jealousy. For I have betrothed you to one husband, that I might present you as a chaste virgin to Christ.

We see this same principle even with the disciples of Jesus. Now no one would dispute they were not the Bride, but when asked why His disciples were not fasting Jesus referred to them as *'friends of the Bridegroom'*:

And Jesus said to them, "Can the friends of the bridegroom mourn as long as the bridegroom is with them? But the days will come when the bridegroom will be taken away from them, and then they will fast". (Matthew 9:15 NKJV).

> *Jesus taught on the need for individual preparation and so He used the parable of the ten virgins to highlight the difference between being wise and foolish.*

QB4 What is the Significance of the Number 10 in the Parable of the Virgins?

When it comes to biblical numerology there is a principle I like to use. That any numbers we consider should only be used to support a principle which already exists in the bible; numbers have a supporting role not a primary one. So, in answer to our question: why were there ten virgins? we need to look at what is already in scripture to see if there is a parallel with the number ten. Well, it just so happens there are a few, but I want to draw our attention to two in particular and then I'll share what I believe is the closest reason for ten virgins. The first parallel is the number ten leading to judgement day. There were ten generations which passed from Adam to Noah when God judged the sin of mankind by sending the great flood, and there are ten virgins which are to be ready for when the Bridegroom comes, which is also the day of the Lord. Jesus himself said:

And as it was in the days of Noah, so it will be also in the days of the Son of Man. (Luke 17:26 NKJV).

The second parallel is the number of ten commandments which represent the marriage covenant given by the Lord to Israel on Mount Sinai. In Leviticus 26:3,12(NET) it reads:

If you walk in my statutes and are sure to obey my commandments .... I will walk among you, and I will be your God and you will be my people.

Whilst these parallels hold interest, I think ultimately the significance of the number ten in this parable is that in Jewish custom ten was and is the minimum required number to form a congregation or assembly which can officiate certain religious ceremonies including reading the marriage blessing. Interestingly Ruth 4:2 gives the account of Boaz assembling ten elders at the city gate to oversee the redemption of Ruth to be his wife. This number ten is when individuals become a collective body and illustrates the corporate nature of the bride, that though she is made up from many individuals, she is one. Paul writes in Romans 12:5[ESV]:

So we, though many, are one body in Christ and individually members of one another.

QB5 Who will Be at the wedding Banquet?

This follows on from the previous question about the ten virgins and whether we are prepared or not when the Bridegroom returns. Now I'm hoping you'll grant me some latitude and allow me to use the virgins, the lamps and the oil symbolically. For example, oil is a well-accepted symbol of the Holy Spirit[7], but Jesus doesn't make this connection directly, it's inferred, and therefore we are making an assumption, nonetheless, it is a reasonable assumption and one that I'm happy to accept. Now in the same manner, to answer our question who will be at the wedding banquet, even though this is hotly debated, I believe it is reasonable to say the virgins can represent those who are saved.[8] After all, they are all expected at the wedding, they are all part of the bridal company, and they are all expecting the Bridegroom to return which reflects their belief.[9]

---

[7] The Spirit of the Lord is upon Me, because He has anointed Me (Luke 4:18 NKJV).
how God anointed Jesus of Nazareth with the Holy Spirit and with power, who went about doing good and healing all who were oppressed by the devil, for God was with Him. (Act 10:38 NKJV).
[8] For I am jealous for you with godly jealousy. For I have betrothed you to one husband, that I may present you as a chaste virgin to Christ. (2 Corinthians 11:2 NKJV).
[9] This is by no means the only interpretation of the parable; I believe Jesus' teaching here relates to Israel, as we shall see later, the wedding

The problem is that the Bridegroom was delayed in coming, and was therefore longer than they expected, so when they had all awoken, the foolish declared their lamps were going out (some translations say have gone out), but either way it shows they had been lit previously which meant they all began with a lamp and with oil. The difference between them was the wise took extra oil in a separate flask. The Greek word used for the lamps going out is *'to quench'*, this same word is found in 1 Thessalonians 5:19(NKJV) where Paul writes:

do not quench the Spirit.

O how we need to be continually filled with the Holy Spirit. Not just once but a daily infilling.

> *There is extra oil for the Bride to help her be ready during the night watch.*

The foolish virgins' lamps had been quenched and they had no oil. Then while they had gone out to buy more oil, the door to the wedding banquet was shut and they were not permitted to enter. Though they pleaded to be let in, the Lord replied: *"I do not know you"*. As controversial as it may be, my answer to our question is that not everyone who is saved and therefore began in the bridal company will be allowed to enter the wedding, but only those who have their lamps lit when the Bridegroom comes. [10]

---

covenant is with Israel, they are expected at the wedding, and are betrothed and waiting for their Husband. But the point I am bringing here is one of individual preparation.

[10] If ascribing this parable to Israel, then we might understand the foolish virgins as those who were not saved.

QB6 What is the Extra Oil?

If our passport into the wedding banquet depends upon us having extra oil so we can keep our lamps lit, then the question we might ask is whether this extra oil is more of what we already have, or is it different in some way? Well to answer that question let's continue with our symbology in the parable of the ten virgins. A central part of this parable is how the lamps that required oil should be lit. Why should it matter whether the virgins had lamps or not? Well, what does a lamp do? It gives off light so the holder can see where they are or where they need to go, and as it was customary for the Bridegroom to come at night the Bridal company needed to have lamps that were lit so they could find their way in the night. The psalmist writes:

Your Word is a lamp to my feet and a light to my path (Psalms 119:105 NKJV).

Isn't this so true? It has been the Word of God that has shown us the way, has given direction in our life, and revealed things we couldn't see before. Yet it was only because the Holy Spirit brought the revelation of what we read and heard in the Word. Yes, it is the Holy Spirit who illuminates the Word so that we are quickened by the living Word in our hearts. Now just before Jesus went to the Cross, He told His disciples in John 16:12-13 (LEB):

I still have many things to say to you, but you are not able to bear them now. 13 But when he—the Spirit of truth—comes, he will guide you into all the truth. For he will not speak on His own authority, but whatever he hears he will speak, and he will proclaim to you the things to come.

This is an interesting verse. It says there were things Jesus didn't share with His disciples. Even in the period of forty days before His ascension where He taught them many things about the Kingdom[11], He still didn't tell them everything, because the verse says when the Holy Spirit comes, *"He will guide them into all truth"*, and even more specifically about the things to come. The revelation of the Word illuminated by the Holy Spirit has helped us to arrive at where we are today. But where we are today is not yet our final destination.

> *The Holy Spirit wants to take us on a journey and is bringing fresh revelation of the Word, to help us see what we have not seen before. There is extra oil for the Bride. The oil is the same Holy Spirit, but the revelation is different, and it's this new light that will help the Bride go further and deeper than she has ever been before: from Salvation to Marriage, from Covenant to Consummation.*

---

[11] Acts 1:3.

QB7 How Does the Bride Get the Extra Oil?

One of the longest chapters in the bible is Genesis 24 which is all about the Bride and typified in this chapter by Rebekah. The account given is after Sarah had died, Abraham summoned His chief servant Eliezer[12] to go and find a wife for his son Isaac from among his own people. So, there are Abraham (meaning father of many), Isaac (who is called the only begotten son)[13] and the chief servant. Here is a picture of the trinity, in which the Father commissions the Holy Spirit to find a wife for His Son. Remember the story? How the chief servant travels to the far country[14], back to the Father's extended family, and asks for a sign in which the suitable Bride will be the one found by the well and offers water for the servant's camels also[15]. When Rebekah fulfilled this requirement of kind service to a stranger, the bible says the servant brought out gifts of gold.[16] Wow, can you imagine that? Rebekah got a lot more than she expected when she showed

---

[12] This is assumed, because the name Eliezer is not given in the chapter, although he is mentioned earlier in Abraham's life in Genesis 15:2.

[13] By faith Abraham, when he was tested, offered up Isaac, and he who had received the promises offered up his only begotten son, (Hebrews 11:17 NKJV).

[14] but you shall go to my country and to my family, and take a wife for my son Isaac. (Genesis 24:4 NKJV).

[15] Genesis 24:12-14.

[16] So it was, when the camels had finished drinking, that the man took a golden nose ring weighing half a shekel, and two bracelets for her wrists weighing ten shekels of gold, (Genesis 24:22 NKJV).

kindness that day. Even though the servant had not explained why he had come he gave gifts. This is a picture of the church at the well. The church has received gifts from the Holy Spirit, without yet hearing the message of the Bride.

This is the first outpouring, the gifts of the Spirit for the church by the well. But the story doesn't end there! Rebekah invites the man back to her home and runs back home to tell her guardian brother Laban all that had happened. And just like Rebekah, those who show respect and kindness to the Holy Spirit begin to position themselves to receive the extra oil. Laban ran out to meet the servant and brought him back to their home.[17] It is here when the servant shared the reason why he had come, how he had come to find a wife for Isaac. Laban accepted the bridal message and released Rebekah to go, saying: *"This is from the lord"*.[18] At which point the servant brought out more gifts including clothes for Rebekah to wear.[19] Here then is the answer to our question, how does the Bride get the extra oil?

> *There is an outpouring by the Holy Spirit which is given*
> *upon accepting the bridal message and agreeing to follow*
> *the Holy Spirit back to the Bridegroom. This is what the*
> *Spirit is saying to the churches today. I have come for the*

---

[17] Now Rebekah had a brother whose name was Laban, and Laban ran out to the man by the well. (Genesis 24:29 NKJV).
So it came to pass, when he saw the nose ring, and the bracelets on his sister's wrists, and when he heard the words of his sister Rebekah, saying, "Thus the man spoke to me," that he went to the man. And there he stood by the camels at the well. (Genesis 24:30 NKJV).
[18] Then Laban and Bethuel answered and said, "The thing comes from the LORD; we cannot speak to you either bad or good." (Genesis 24:50 NKJV).
[19] Then the servant brought out jewellery of silver, jewellery of gold, and clothing, and gave them to Rebekah. He also gave precious things to her brother and to her mother. (Genesis 24:53 NKJV).

Bride. I have gifts and clothes to help her to get ready, but you must not detain me on my quest.[20] *The Bride belongs to the bridegroom, there is nothing that we can do to beautify her or make her ready in the natural, it is the Holy Spirit who will enable the Bride to get ready when she receives the extra oil.*

---

[20] This is what Laban tried to do on the following morning. Who knows what he thought during the night as he marvelled of his guest and the gifts that were given? But the point is getting comfortable or holding onto the current blessing can lead to reluctance in letting the Bride go! We must take heed, for the Lord is zealous for His Bride and will not take kindly to anyone interfering with His wedding plans!

QB8 Will You Go with This Man?

The Bridal message the Holy Spirit is bringing to the church today is a challenge of radical reform that confronts and threatens to change much of what we have understood about the church. Our perspectives, preferences, personalities, and programming must all give way to a vastly superior paradigm. The bridal paradigm isn't asking to be squeezed onto our already crowded bookshelves along with other doctrines to be referenced occasionally, but it is the very bookshelf upon which everything else must either find a place to fit or be discarded altogether. The bridal paradigm demands a reformation at the core of who we are, it is our identity that is under review here. It is not a refreshing or even another revival that is required. Over the years the church has had many and yet still remains asking for more. Though we thank the Lord for those we've had, what is needed here goes deeper than a refreshing or revival, what is needed is an awakening to our highest identity.

> *There is something deeply hidden away in every child of God which resonates with the Bridal message because the Spirit of God placed the Bridal DNA within us all when we were born again.*

It merely needs to be awakened like a planted seed waiting to be watered, or like the sleeping beauty, the Bride is being romanced in the wilderness with kisses from the Son. Now here is the challenge confronting the church and its leadership today. We could say that just as Laban was looking after his sister Rebekah, so the leaders of the church today have a custodian role for the Bride which is a temporary assignment to nurture and provide for her until the time comes for her to leave.[21] Now after Laban had originally accepted the bridal message and agreed to release Rebekah, by the time the morning had come, he had changed his mind and wanted to slow down the whole affair. The account describes how the servant became angry and warned: *"Hinder me not since the Lord has prospered my journey".* [22]

Once the Holy Spirit brings the bridal message we must not stand in His way; the Lord is jealous for His Bride! The word jealous means fiercely protective of one's rights or possessions, and this is how the Lord is over His Bride. Laban quickly retreats and suggests *'let's ask the girl'*, by calling her a girl, he is emphasising her age, suggesting she is not ready. O how mistaken we are when we think we know better than the Lord concerning His Bride. So here is the question we must all answer, it is the question put to Rebekah that day:

Will you go with this man? (Genesis 24:58 NKJV).

Will you forsake the comfortability of what you know and even those around you into the unknown journey of the Bride? Will you come to embrace the message that demands an answer and align yourself with your bridal identity? It's time for the Bride to arise, it's time to

---

[21] This is an important point which John the Baptist understood well when he said "The Bride belongs to the Bridegroom The friend who attends the bridegroom waits and listens for him and is full of joy when he hears the bridegroom's voice. That joy is mine, and it is now complete." (John 3:29 NIV) Leaders take note, if you have been appointed to office, then it is as a 'friend of the Bridegroom', and like John the Baptist said of Jesus "He must increase, but I must decrease" (John 3:30 NKJV).
[22] Genesis 24:56.

receive the extra oil. Let us respond like Rebekah did who answered simply but decisively:

I will go.

QB9 Does the Bridal Paradigm Change My Relationship with the Father?

Tbere is rarely something more beautiful than a changed life, like the story of the prodigal son, who from spiritual destitution and being alone is restored back into the Father's house. In the loving embrace of arms that stretched out wide to greet him; pain, fears, and failures were washed away in the overwhelming love his father had toward him. So it is also for us. We too have come to know the Father's love, and through our relationship with Him are finding the place of healing, confidence, identity and all the blessings of what it means to be a child of God. This was Jesus' heart for us, that we would know the Father and His great love for us. John puts it beautifully when he writes in his first letter 1 John 3:1:

Behold what manner of love the Father has bestowed upon us, that we should be called the children of God, for that is what we are.

It is quite clear: the focus of Jesus first coming was to restore us into a loving relationship with the Father. It is no wonder then, there is a natural concern when considering the implications of the Bridal Paradigm and how this may affect our relationship with the Father. And it should! Because it reflects our love for Him. But let us be reassured He will always be our Father and being awakened by a new romance with the Son is in no way a replacement of our love for

Him. Indeed it remains necessary for us to remain in the Father's house because it is here we grow into the maturity that is capable of marriage and this is the Father's heart for us that we should mature and be ready as a Bride for His Son.

> *It is only because we are first children of the Father, that we are able to be a Bride for the Son. And just as it is not possible to come to the Father except through the Son, (John 14:6) neither is it possible to come to the Son except through the Father.*

When Jesus prayed in Gethsemane, He said:

I pray for those whom You have given Me, for they are Yours. (John 17:9).

It is the Father who gives us to the Son. Let us then continue to grow into maturity which comes through a right relationship with the Father but let us also embrace how that maturity is one which prepares us for the deepest love of all. What glory awaits us of which we barely conceive, yet the Spirit bears witness of what we are now is only the foretaste of what shall be. I will close with a favourite scripture of mine in 1 John 3:2:

Beloved, now we are children of God; and it has not yet been revealed what we shall be, but we know that when He is revealed, we shall be like Him, for we shall see Him as He is.

QB10 Why Should the Bride Call Come Now? (Part 1)

J ohn writes in 1 John 3:2:

Beloved, now we are children of God; and it has not yet been revealed what we shall be, but we know that when He is revealed, we shall be like Him, for we shall see Him as He is.

John is saying though we are now the children of God, there is so much more, for what we shall be, has not yet been revealed. The word *'revealed'* means something previously unknown or a secret - to make known to others, something (or someone) which is hidden away, to make it appear so it is plainly recognised and thoroughly understood. Paul writes:

For now, we see in a mirror dimly but then face to face, now I know in part, but then I shall fully know, even as I am fully known (1 Corinthians 13:12 ESV).

Whilst there remain things which we will not know or understand fully until our glorification takes place when Jesus returns, yet it is true now that what no eye has seen or ear heard, what no heart of man has imagined of what God has prepared for those who love Him, those things can be revealed by the Spirit which searches even the very depths of God[23]. We are able to know now in part of what

---

[23] 1 Corinthians 2:9-10.

we shall be then. Indeed, we must have this revelation of what we shall be, so we can align ourselves with God's heart and intentions towards us now, for we must prepare now for what shall be then. Not only the revelation but also the quickening of this transformation process of who we are in Christ, is a work of the Spirit of God within the yielded believer. But the role of the Holy Spirit has not ended with either the revelation or the outworking thereof, for the Holy Spirit also testifies with our spirit of this great work He has done in us that we may know in full assurance of who we are, and in knowing we might appropriate and take possession of our identity in Christ. Let me summarise these steps and work of the Holy Spirit within us:

- Step 1: The Holy Spirit brings revelation of who we are.

- Step 2: The Holy Spirit quickens this work within us.

- Step 3: The Holy Spirit testifies with our spirit what He has done.

In Romans 8:16 Paul writes:

The Spirit Himself bears witness with our spirit that we are children of God

Once the Spirit has brought revelation, transformation (quickening) and testimony (witness) of His great work, it activates a cry within us that agrees with the work of the Holy Spirit within us. For we have received the Spirit of adoption by which we cry: *"Abba Father!"* [24]

---

[24] For you did not receive the spirit of bondage again to fear, but you received the Spirit of adoption by whom we cry out, "Abba, Father." (Romans 8:15 NKJV).

- Step 4: We verbally call out a witness of this internalised truth about our identity.

All this pertains to our identity as children of God. But it has also been revealed by the same Spirit that we are not only children of the Father, but we are also the Bride of His Son Jesus.

> *The same Spirit by which we have been born again into adoption as sons is the same Spirit by which we have been brought into betrothal as the Bride. Furthermore, this same Spirit which bears witness we are the sons of God also bears witness in our spirit we are the Bride.*

Now here is the answer to our question, why should the Bride call come now? Because just as the correct response for us as children of God is to cry *"Abba Father"*, and this cry activated in us by the *'Spirit of Adoption'*, so also the correct response for us as the Bride of Jesus Christ is to cry *"Come"*, and this cry has been activated within us by the *'Spirit of Betrothal'*[25]. This call for the Lord to come is there in each of us and is what needs to be released so we can align ourselves with who we are and appropriate our Bridal identity so we can begin to prepare. Maranatha.

> *By the Spirit of Adoption, we cry "Abba, Father", by the Spirit of Betrothal we cry "Come".*

---

[25] The Spirit of Betrothal is not explicit in scripture, but I use this term in the manner in which Paul describes the 'Spirit of Adoption' as a recognition of the Spirit's work within the child of God.

QB11 Why Should the Bride Call Come Now? (Part 2)

The verse:

> The Spirit and the Bride say "Come!"
> (Revelation 22:17).

is familiar to the church and yet as a whole is not seen as something that requires any particular response or application today, but rather is seen as a statement of what will be when Jesus returns. After all, how can the Bride call "Come" if she is not yet ready? Can the Bride only pray this prayer once she is fully dressed? Or have we missed something which has major significance and implications for the church today?

In Greek *'Come'* is the word *'erchomai'* meaning *'the coming of someone; to come from one place to another and used of persons arriving and those returning; to appear; make one's appearance, or to come before the public.'* This is the word used in Revelation 22:17. But in total the word *'erchomai'* is actually written seven times within this final chapter. Biblically, the number seven is accepted as a number of perfection and completeness. It is written three times when Jesus says He is coming quickly in verses 7,12 and 20. Then it is also written three times in verse 17, which reads:

And the Spirit and the Bride say, Come. And let him who hears say, Come. And let him who is thirsty come.

That is a total of six times so far, and then the closing prayer and benediction of all scripture is made by John who responds to Jesus saying He is coming:

Amen, Come Lord Jesus. [26]

Our Bibles close with this call for Jesus to come, the word *'erchomai'* now written seven times! But on closer inspection, even though *'erchomai'* is written seven times, it is actually used eight times and the number eight is also significant as it is the number of new beginnings. So how can it be written seven times but used eight? Well amongst the recitations of *'Come'*, on one occasion it is a joint prayer of agreement. In Revelation 22:17 it says:

the Spirit and the Bride say "Come!"

It is written once but used twice by both the Holy Spirit and the Bride.

> *This is the ultimate prayer of agreement, for when the Bride calls 'Come' she is agreeing with the Spirit who has always been saying 'Come' and it is like a portal opened between heaven and earth because there has been a wonderful alignment between the two realms, a convergence, a unification of heart.*

We should need no further rationale when we realise this is the written record, the closing prayer of scripture. The call to *'Come'* is not therefore an option for the Bride, she is compelled, for she is responding from a heart that has been quickened by the Spirit within her calling come. John closes with this call. Let him who has ears to

---

[26] He who testifies to these things says, "Surely I am coming quickly." Amen. Even so, come, Lord Jesus! (Revelation 22:20 NKJV).

hear, let him say *'Come'.*[27] If we listen deep inside our spirit, we will hear this cry, let it therefore be released and let us join together to ask the Lord to *'Come'.*

---

[27] John writes in Revelation 22:17 'let him who hears say "Come!"'. One might ask hear what? And my answer would be what the Spirit is saying to the churches. This is the witness of the Spirit in the church today, the Bride is waking up around the nations of the world because the Spirit has come for the Bride. Those with their spiritual ears and eyes open will have experienced this already, and if we have heard, then here is our instruction: 'let him who hears say "Come!"'

QB12 Why Should the Bride Call Come Now? (Part 3)

In the final chapter of our Bibles, Revelation 22, Jesus is on centre stage and talking directly to us through the words of the prophecy given to John. Each time Jesus speaks it reveals something important either about the manner of His coming or the glory in which He will come. Like the closing argument and summation in a courtroom, where emphasis is given on the main points to be considered and a justification of what the correct response or outcome should be, we can look at this chapter in a similar way.

> *What were the last recorded words of Jesus in the Bible? Because whatever they were set the whole context of how the church should live, what should be its vision, and what should be its heartbeat.*

The closing words of Jesus is embedded within the DNA of the church today. So what were our Lord's final words? In Revelation 22:20 Jesus says:

"Surely I am coming quickly (or soon)" and John replies "Amen, Even So, Come Lord Jesus".

This is the correct response and reflects John's heart for His Lord. This is John who was known as *'the disciple whom Jesus loved'*[28], John who witnessed the miracles, the humanity and the deity of Jesus whilst upon the earth. John who stood at the foot of the cross and took Mary the Mother of Jesus into his home[29], and for more than sixty years[30] after Jesus ascended back to Heaven to sit at the right hand of the Father, had lived his life as the apostle of love, and now in his old age was exiled on Patmos[31]. John knew Jesus intimately perhaps more than any other. He knew Jesus' heart for us, and he also knew the only answer for a victorious church, was for it to be ready as the Bride. Only then would Jesus come back again to establish His throne personally and geographically in Jerusalem.

It's what Heaven is waiting for; for the Wife to make herself ready. Not a Kingdom Now perspective through a surrogate church representing Jesus on earth while He remained in Heaven, oh no, such post-millennial thinking was never a thought in John or the

---

[28] It should be noted that not all agree John was the disciple Jesus loved, but it is my view and that held by the early church fathers. The phrase 'the disciple who Jesus loved' is found six times, all within the Gospel of John. It is this disciple who is attributed for writing John's Gospel. 'This is the disciple who testifies of these things, and wrote these things; and we know that his testimony is true.' (John 21:24 NKJV).

[29] When Jesus therefore saw His mother, and the disciple whom He loved standing by, He said to His mother, "Woman, behold your son!" Then He said to the disciple, "Behold your mother!" And from that hour that disciple took her to his own home. (John 19:26,27 NKJV).

[30] Historians generally agree Jesus died around AD30 - AD33, similarly, Revelation was written around AD95, meaning the time between John, meaning the time between John with Jesus at the Cross and the Revelation received on Patmos was around 60 years.

[31] Revelation 1:9.

early church fathers[32]. No, it was only by Jesus' actual bodily return as the King of Kings and Lord of Lords, crowned with many crowns, which would finally overthrow the kingdoms of darkness, destroy the antichrist and the false prophet[33], and establish a millennial reign in which Satan would be bound for a thousand years[34]. This is the *'blessed hope'*[35] we should hold so dear to our hearts, the hope of His glorious appearing, that Jesus who promised will come back, shall return soon.

When Jesus said He was coming quickly, what else could John say? What else can we say, if Jesus says He is coming soon, what should our response be? Should we say, *"not yet Lord, I haven't finished what I wanted to do, not yet Lord the church is still growing, not yet Lord we haven't established your kingdom in every nation and sector of society."*? No, the call to *'Come'* is the right and honouring response that can only be made by the Bride. Did you notice the Bible doesn't say the Spirit and the Church say *'Come!'* But it is the Spirit and the Bride who say *'Come!'*.

> *The church without her bridal identity will continue to go through an endless cycle of reformation and reset*[36] *until*

---

[32] When I refer to the early church fathers, I mean those within a generation of the New Testament writers (e.g. Justin Martyr AD100-165), and not the likes of Augustine (AD354-430) or Origen (AD184-253), who took a less literal view of scripture and allegorised much of eschatology. Such persuasions gave rise to post-millennialism and amillennialism. This is a simplified view, the details of which are beyond the scope of this text.

[33] Revelation 19:20.

[34] Revelation 20:1-3.

[35] Titus 2:13.

[36] There is a correlation between identity and destiny. If one does not know who they are or where they are headed it would not be difficult to see how that would impede their progress.

she can finally agree with the Spirit and call 'Come' as the Bride.

It is this call to *'Come'*, which breaks that cycle and aligns us with our destiny, and it is this call Heaven is waiting to hear as a sure sign the Bride is getting ready[37], and more than anything else her desire is for Him.

---

[37] I believe there is a shift of focus that needs to take place from calling for the Holy Spirit to Come to calling for Jesus to Come. This was a key part of the founding vision I received that birthed the Call2Come movement. I saw the longing of Jesus' heart to hear His Bride call for Him. When Father and Son look upon the earth and they hear the church calling for the Holy Spirit to come rather than for Jesus, how does that make him feel? What message are we conveying, what exposure of our heart? Don't get me wrong, yes, of course, it is right and necessary to ask for the Holy Spirit, that's not the point I'm making. But whilst the church continues to pray for another outpouring of the Holy Spirit and not for the Lord Jesus Christ to 'Come', one must ask the question why? In the founding vision I saw Jesus turn to the Father and ask "Father can you hear them? They are asking for the Holy Spirit to come, when are they going to ask for Me?" But O how wonderful, as the Bride begins to call "Come", I saw the joy in His eyes as He asked the Father again "Father can you hear them?" But this time it was for Him, and Jesus looked longingly to His Father and said, "Father can I go?" and Father smiled saying, "Soon My Son, but this is what we will do. Let us send the Holy Spirit one more time, to help her to get dressed!" That was the founding vision I received and remains the heartbeat of Call2Come. I believe there is an outpouring of the Holy Spirit to come in these last days. An outpouring the church has never experienced. It is one reserved for the Bride, and it will not come by asking for the Holy Spirit, but for the Lord Jesus Christ Himself to 'Come'. That's why we need to call "Come" now so that we can get ready. So that we can break the endless cycle of reset, cross over the threshold of our Bridal identity and receive the last outpouring of the Holy Spirit reserved for the Bride.

QB13 Could Jesus Return At Any Time?

In Revelation 22, Jesus declared three times He was coming back quickly. The word *'quickly'* in Greek *'tachy'* ('ta-who') means speedily, suddenly, without delay or soon. In verse 7 Jesus said:

Behold, I am coming quickly! Blessed is he who keeps the words of the prophecy of this book.

Then in verse 12, He said:

And behold, I am coming quickly, and My reward is with Me, to give to everyone according to his work,

Then finally in verse 20, Jesus said:

He who testifies to these things says, "Surely I am coming quickly."

This is the manner in which Jesus will return; when He comes, as He surely will, He will come quickly. When the time set by the Father is fulfilled, He will not delay. Presently Jesus is received in Heaven as it says in Acts 3:21 *'until the restoration of all things'*, but when that time comes, the nature of His return will be one of great speed, just like lightning, so shall the glory of His appearing be[38]. This quick return sets the spiritual climate in which we have been living for the last

---

[38] For as the lightning comes from the east and flashes to the west, so also will the coming of the Son of Man be. (Mattew 24:27 NKJV).

two thousand years, that Jesus will come back speedily. But notice here there is a difference between a quick return and an imminent one. Though Jesus says He's coming back quickly, doesn't mean His return is imminent, as in the sense Jesus could return at any moment unexpectedly, for Jesus also gives clear instruction about the signs of His coming. It is true we will not know the hour as in Matthew 24:36 which reads:

But of that day and hour no one knows, not even the angels of heaven, but My Father only

But though we may not know the day or hour of His return, Jesus uses the parable of the fig tree to describe that when you see the *'things'* He told them, taking place, then to know this is the season of His return. Listen to what Luke writes in chapter 21:

28 "Now when these things begin to take place, straighten up and raise your heads, because your redemption is drawing near." 29 And he told them a parable: "Look at the fig tree, and all the trees. 30 As soon as they come out in leaf, you see for yourselves and know that the summer is already near. 31 So also, when you see these things taking place, you know that the kingdom of God is near."
(Luke 21:28-31 ESV).

> **The Bible doesn't teach an imminent return[39]. Though it says you won't know the day or hour, doesn't mean it could be any day or hour.**

---

[39] Though this is the belief of many sincere Christians, there is no explicit verse to support this view. It is normally a supposition based upon a pre-tribulation perspective.

Yes, Jesus will return like a thief in the night which will catch those in darkness by surprise, but only when certain criteria have first been fulfilled. The only return the Bible teaches is when He returns in great glory known as the Day of the Lord[40], which Paul writes should not be a surprise to us, because we are children of the light[41]. Jesus taught us to watch and pray, for there are signs which will herald when the day of His coming is near, and He will return exactly in the way He said He would, in the way which is recorded for us in His Word, so we will know. And the final recorded requirement, the one that all Heaven is waiting for is found in Revelation 19:7:

Let us be glad and rejoice and give Him glory, for the marriage of the Lamb has come, and His wife has made herself ready.

---

[40] As we shall see later, there is more to unpack here, but the point I'm making is there is no secret coming before the Lord's appearing on the Day of the Lord that is supported from scripture.
[41] 1 Thessalonians 5:1-5.

QB14 I Am the Alpha and the Omega

If the final chapter of Revelation is like the closing argument or summation in a courtroom, in which the defence and prosecution present their fundamental argument and main points of the case, then these closing words of Jesus in the Bible present the emphasis and context of the time we are living in now and sets the tone and agenda for what will follow.

There is however a fundamental difference from the courtroom analogy. Because in a courtroom after the summation, it is down to the jury and judge to deliberate on the verdict and what the final ruling should be, but in the case of our Lord's return: the Final Judgement, the Millennium, the New Heaven and Earth, and the Wedding of the Lamb; all these future events are not subject to third party scrutiny or the deliberation of man. Indeed, these things have already been ruled upon, and the verdict written in the Heavenly record before creation ever burst forth when the Lord spoke the words: *"let there be light"*. For the Lord has known the end from the beginning and has determined the glorious outcome that awaits us ahead of time.

Regardless of man's opinion, political machinations, humanistic appetite, and flagrant violation of God's statutes, the Lord is in absolute control of future events. Man may try to erect his Tower of Babel like Nimrod in defiance of God and rebellion against His judgement through the flood, but there is no empire that man, the ancient dragon, or the antichrist can build that will stand against the coming of the Lord[42]. This was the summation given by our Lord Jesus Christ. His closing declaration when He said:

I am the Alpha and the Omega, the First and the Last, the Beginning and the End. (Revelation 22:13 ESV).

It was an unequivocal, undeniable, unchangeable and indisputable statement of truth. He doesn't yield to our agendas, our philosophies or our beliefs of what is or isn't true. He stands before the entire world and says: "*I Am*"[43]. No man on Earth or power of darkness in heavenly places can change who He is, or His Eternal plan set in motion before time began. He defies all powers, thrones, and Kingdoms, for His name is higher than any other.

He is the Alpha. He is before all things and in Him and through Him all things were created and have their being. He was eternally existent and coequal with the Father and has not changed in who He is, and yet His form did change, so He might forever be the mediator of a New Covenant, and the propitiation of our sins through His own sacrifice in human flesh. This is the One who is speaking to us in

---

[42] He shall speak pompous words against the Most High, Shall persecute the saints of the Most High, And shall intend to change times and law. Then the saints shall be given into his hand For a time and times and half a time. (Daniel 7:25 NKJV).
The enemy will intend (think) to change the times and law, we cannot know to what effect his attempts shall have only the certainty that God is Sovereign, and He is the One who sets the time clock for all eternity, past, present and future.
And He changes the times and the seasons; He removes kings and raises up kings; He gives wisdom to the wise And knowledge to those who have understanding. (Daniel 2:21 NKJV).
[43] Jesus said to them, "Most assuredly, I say to you, before Abraham was, I AM." (John 8:58 NKJV).

this final chapter as He makes His closing speech, for He says, I Jesus have sent my angel to bring my testimony to you, that I Am.

Jesus is not only the Alpha, but He is also the Omega. His is the first word and His will be the last. He will have the final say. The summation of all things is Christ Himself. His closing argument is not with a rationale appealing to reason, but a declaration of who He is as the Alpha and Omega[44]. He is His own self-existent statement of truth that demands respect and cannot be refuted, those who do not yield cannot change their fate for they will give their account why they did not believe or refuse to accept their only hope of salvation, and those who do believe and accept the Alpha and Omega, will be those who join with the Spirit and respond by saying '*Come*!'.

---

[44] When Jesus declares He is the Alpha and the Omega, there is little room for any other opinion about His deity and His co-equality with God the Father. The Bride must be strong on this point, for today there is all manner of heresy and error about who Jesus was and is. As John 1:1,2 reads 'In the beginning was the Word, and the Word was with God, and the Word was God, He was with God in the beginning.' This equality between the Father and the Son can also be seen clearly through the statement "I am the Alpha and the Omega", because in Revelation 21:6 the Father also calls Himself the Alpha and the Omega.

QB15 I Am the Root and Offspring of David

We have been looking at the importance of Jesus' final words before our Bibles close with the apostle John's response who calls upon Jesus to come. These words are important because what Jesus says here consolidates and focuses our understanding of who He is and why He's coming back. Jesus as the Alpha and Omega is a powerful statement of His absolute deity and authority above all things, it is also a name the Father gives Himself in Revelation 21:6,7, we know on this occasion it is the Father speaking because He refers to those who overcome as His sons. So this name of the Alpha and the Omega demonstrates Jesus' complete harmony and oneness with the Father. Hebrews 1:3[NIV] speaking of Jesus says this:

The Son is the radiance of God's glory and the exact representation of his being, sustaining all things by his powerful word. After he had provided purification for sins, he sat down at the right hand of the Majesty in heaven.

When Jesus says: *"I Am the Alpha and the Omega"*, He is stating the truth of who He is. He is able to be the Alpha and Omega, the First and the Last, Beginning and the End, because He is One with the Father, and He is worthy to hold the highest office because:

He is 'the Lamb who was slain from the foundation of the world' (Revelation 13:8).

Jesus as the Alpha and the Omega is God in human form, but not the Adamic form from the dust, but the glorified form that awaits us also on His return. This first statement of being the Alpha and the Omega sets the foundation for the second when Jesus said:

I am the root and the offspring of David
(Revelation 22:16).

> *The first statement is one of His eternal nature; the second is one of His eternal office. It is because He is the 'Alpha and Omega' that He is able to be the 'root and offspring of David'.*

Jesus' was the first throne, and His will be the last. Kingdoms rise and fall, leaders too, all at His sovereign hand. David was King because Jesus had always been King, the pre-existing King who reigns with the Father as the Son of God, but now as the offspring of David, He is coming as the Son of Man to reign from Mount Zion, bringing Heaven and Earth together under one Sovereign Head who is Christ. In Revelation 11:15[ESV] we read:

Then the seventh angel blew his trumpet, and there were loud voices in heaven, saying, "The kingdom of this world has become the kingdom of our Lord and of his Christ, and he shall reign forever and ever."

When Jesus said He was *"the root and the offspring of David"*, He was saying *"I am the fulfilment of all the messianic prophecies of a future king and glorious kingdom"*. 1 Kings 9:5 reads:

Then I will establish the throne of your kingdom over Israel for ever, as I promised your father David saying, "You will never fail to have a man on the throne of Israel."

Jesus is returning to earth and will reign from Mount Zion[45] forever, in doing so, He is fulfilling the promises made to David and Israel for a future King and Kingdom. Is not the One who died for the sins of the world worthy to be its King also? There is no one else like Him, no one else who is worthy to take the scroll and to open its seals[46], no one else who is both God and Man in which He is able to bring Heaven and Earth together in one new glorious Kingdom over which He shall reign. Behold your King, the King of all Kings is coming, and

Of the increase of his government and of peace there will be no end, on the throne of David and over his kingdom, to establish it and to uphold it with justice and with righteousness from this time forth and forevermore. The zeal of the LORD of hosts will do this. (Isaiah 9:7 [ESV]).

---

[45] Great is the Lord, and greatly to be praised. In the city of our God, in His holy mountain. Beautiful in elevation, the joy of the whole earth, is Mount Zion on the sides of the north, the city of the great King. (Psalms 48:1,2 NKJV).

[46] But one of the elders said to me, "Do not weep. Behold, the Lion of the tribe of Judah, the Root of David, has prevailed to open the scroll and to loose its seven seals." (Revelation 5:5 NKJV).

QB16 The Bright Morning Star

When Jesus first came as the incarnate Son of God, born of the Virgin Mary, there was a star that appeared in the east[47] to signify His arrival. It was a sign in the heavens given by the Father to mark the arrival of His Son. Those who understood how to interpret the signs for the coming of the Lord were given the means by which they might follow the star and it led them to Bethlehem, where they worshipped the One born King of the Jews and bowed down to present to Him their offerings of gold, frankincense and myrrh.[48] Yet these wise men were not Jewish but from the lands in the East, and as John writes:

He came to His own, and His own did not receive Him.
(John 1:11 NKJV).

In meekness and majesty, as a baby laid in a manger in humble attire, was born the Star that even the pagan prophet Balaam foresaw when he prophesied concerning the Messiah in Numbers 24:17[NKJV]:

I see him, but not now; I behold him, but not near: a star shall come out of Jacob, and a sceptre shall rise out of Israel;

Yet when Jesus returns, it will not be in obscurity or without the observation of the entire world. On His First Coming, His own did not receive Him, but when Jesus comes again,

---

[47] Matthew 2:2.
[48] Matthew 2:1-12.

they will look on Me whom they pierced. Yes, they will mourn for Him as one mourns for his only son,
(Zechariah 12:10 [NKJV]).

On His first coming, a star went before Him and was noticed by only a few, on His second He will be that star, and the whole world will witness His arrival. Jesus said, *"I am the Bright Morning Star"*[49]. The term *'Morning Star'* is significant and is known to astronomers as the planet Venus. Apart from the sun and the moon, Venus is the brightest object in the sky. The reason it is called the morning star is because, at certain times of the year, Venus rises above the horizon to greet the dawn whilst it is still dark, as a precursor to the rising of the sun which heralds a new day is dawning. This is the description Jesus uses for Himself as the *'Morning Star'*, His coming signifies a new day is dawning, and night is ending. His coming will usher in a new era in which He will reign forever and ever.

Worthy of note is that the term *'morning star'* was also used of Lucifer in Isaiah 14:12[NIV]:

How you have fallen from heaven, morning star, son of the dawn! You have been cast down to the earth, you who once laid low the nations!

But there is a great difference between the Lord and Lucifer - a chasm so great that one cannot be reconciled to the other. Lucifer was a created light, so given to radiate the glory of God. But Jesus is no created light, for He is the Light, the Light of the world. A light so great not an infinite number of lights combined could compare to His radiance. That is why He is not only the *'Morning Star'*, but

---

[49] Revelation 22:16.

Jesus is the *'Bright Morning Star'*. Paul writes in Thessalonians concerning the coming of the Lord saying:

And then the lawless one will be revealed, whom the Lord will consume with the breath of his mouth and destroy with the brightness of His coming
(2 Thessalonians 2:8 [NKJV]).

His brightness will dispel the greatest of darkness, which no power of Hell will be able to stand or hold Him back. His brightness will expose all counterfeit light and herald a new day, the Millennial Reign, in which we as His Glorious Bride shall radiate His glory as we reign together with Him.

QB17 Alleluia, Alleluia, Alleluia, Alleluia

The final song recorded for us in the Bible is found in Revelation 19. It is the great showstopper, the finale, the masterpiece which until this point has never been able to have been sung, because in the outworking of God's Eternal Plan there remain just a few final pages to be turned. But there will come a time, when history will reach its climax, like the final chapter of a good book, in which everything comes together in a glorious ending where the villains are apprehended, and the hero conquers all. This is where we find this final song, as it bridges the gap between the old dispensation and the new, and its key is '*Alleluia.*'

The first '*Alleluia*' is in verse 1 which reads:

After these things I heard a loud voice of a great multitude in heaven, saying, "Alleluia! Salvation and glory and honour and power belong to the Lord our God!" (Revelation 19:1 NKJV).

For me, this multitude represents those saved from all nations, tribes, peoples and tongues. We have here an early glimpse of the Bride, not yet fully revealed but her praise is loud and exuberant. John refers to this multitude previously in Revelation 7:9,10 who also say:

Salvation belongs to our God who sits on the throne, and to the Lamb!

Her song of praise continues in verses 2 and 3 saying:

For true and righteous are His judgments, because He has judged the great harlot who corrupted the earth with her fornication; and He has avenged on her the blood of His servants shed by her. Again they said, "Alleluia! Her smoke rises up forever and ever!"

This second '*Alleluia*' celebrates the fall of Babylon as previously instructed in chapter 18:20[NIV]:

Rejoice over her, you heavens! Rejoice, you people of God! Rejoice, apostles and prophets! For God has judged her with the judgment she imposed on you.

As in chapter 7:12 so also here in chapter 19, we find it is the Bride in waiting who leads the Alleluia chorus which is then affirmed with the third '*Alleluia*' in verse 4:

And the twenty-four elders and the four living creatures fell down and worshiped God who sat on the throne, saying, "Amen! Alleluia!"

All this praise builds to a great climax and fourth '*Alleluia*' in verses 6 and 7. Verse 6 reads:

And I heard, as it were, the voice of a great multitude, as the sound of many waters and as the sound of mighty thunder, saying, "Alleluia! For the Lord God Omnipotent reigns!"

Here we have also a great multitude similar to those in verse 1 only here we are given a definition of them in the preceding verse which describes them as '*all you His servants and those who fear Him, both small and great*'. Like the build-up of a song in a choir, when at last on the final chorus, all members join together to bring a unified expression at the highest volume possible, so now it is time for all God's servants, both small and great to participate. O how the angels have longed for this moment, having served Almighty God through the ages, having been His servants and carried out His commands, having witnessed Satan and a third of their number fall like lightning, should now join the chorus with the ultimate expression of highest praise saying: *"Alleluia! For the Lord God Omnipotent reigns!"*

It is of no coincidence that this unifying and repeated word *'Alleluia'* is transliterated from the Hebrew language and means *'praise the Lord'*. Alleluia is only found four times in the New Testament and each occurrence is found here. This is the praise language of Israel[50], and Heaven and Earth shall join together to sing her song of the Lord when she finally comes into her salvation and destiny. That's why the final line of this most wonderful song ends with these words in verse 7:

Let us be glad and rejoice and give Him glory, for the marriage of the Lamb has come, and His wife has made herself ready. (Revelation 19:7 NKJV).

---

[50] This is an important point, for Israel shall be saved at this point, though not all Israel as we shall see later in our study.

QB18 How Many Wives Does God Have?

There is a large debate over whether God divorced Israel, often quoting from Jeremiah 3:8 or Hosea 1, but great care is needed in our exegesis to understand what actually took place. At this point in history, Israel was divided into two houses or kingdoms: there was the Northern Kingdom (known as Israel), and the Southern Kingdom (known as Judah). The Lord appeals to the Northern Kingdom of Israel and in Jeremiah 3:8 the prophet writes:

Then I saw that for all the causes for which backsliding Israel had committed adultery, I had put her away and given her a certificate of divorce; yet her treacherous sister Judah did not fear, but went and played the harlot also.

At first glance, it would appear God did divorce Israel, for the passage says He had *'given her a certificate of divorce'*. Yet when we read further on in the same passage in verse 14 we find how the Lord considers Himself still married to her:

"Return, O backsliding children," says the LORD; "for I am married to you. I will take you, one from a city and two from a family, and I will bring you to Zion." (Jeremiah 3:14).

What are we to make of this? Is the Lord still married or not to Israel at this point in time? When Israel divided into two houses, did He then have two wives? Was the Northern Kingdom a wife and the Southern Kingdom another wife? Well, how many betrothals took place on Sinai? There was just one; one wedding between the Lord and Israel. Even though later she divided politically into two, God's covenant remained with Israel as a whole - it was their corporate identity, as One people, who the Lord entered into a covenant relationship with, not with their divisions but their corporate identity as a whole.

> *Therefore, even though the nation of Israel divided politically into two, God didn't then have two wives. In the same way, He doesn't accommodate our divisions and have a separate covenant for each. No, God will always only have one wife, and therefore there will always only be one wedding covenant, one wedding contract.*

The fact is when the northern tribes had torn themselves away from the south, they were not only divorcing (which means separating) themselves from Judah but were also divorcing (or separating) themselves from the Lord and from the covenant which defined their relationship with the Lord as their Husband. Significantly, they then erected statues of Baal in Samaria, the capital of the Northern Kingdom. (The word Ba 'al means husband or master).

When we step out of unity with each other into divisions or plurality we endanger the very covenant relationship by which we are consecrated unto the Lord, for at the heart of that covenant is the glory of oneness. The essential nature of the Bride is that she is one. Is Christ divided? Is there from Him plurality, divisions or even denominations? No! If we are truly in Christ, then we are also truly one with each other. Is this not the enduring message of the bread we share, that we partake of one body, though we are many? How many wives does God have? There is but one. There has only ever been one. He fell in love with her and remains in love with her still.

He has not forsaken her and gone with another, no! His love for her is eternal. Yes she is Israel, but not the Israel of man, but the Israel of God (Galatians 6:16), which includes all those who have come into the New Covenant, both Jew and Gentile. This is a key point when we consider what it means *'the wife has made herself ready'*, that she has not only embraced her bridal identity with the Lord, but also her corporate identity with one another.

QB19 The New Covenant Fulfils an Old Promise

Every marriage begins with a covenant, an exchange of promises and wedding vows made by each partner to the other. This is what took place on Mount Sinai between Israel and Jehovah. There are many scriptural references which highlight the Lord as a Husband to Israel His wife.

"For the LORD has called you like a wife deserted and grieved in spirit, like a wife of youth when she is cast off", says your God. "For a brief moment I deserted you, but with great compassion I will gather you. In overflowing anger for a moment I hid my face from you, but with everlasting love I will have compassion on you", says the LORD, your Redeemer. (Isaiah 54:6-8 ESV).

"Behold, the days are coming", says the LORD, "when I will make a new covenant with the house of Israel and with the house of Judah- not according to the covenant that I made with their fathers in the day that I took them by the hand to lead them out of the land of Egypt, My covenant which they broke, though I was a husband to them", says the LORD. "But this is the covenant that I will make with the house of Israel after those days", says the LORD: "I will put My law in their minds, and write it on their hearts; and I will be their God, and they shall be My people." (Jeremiah 31:31-33 NKJV).

Did you notice something very important in this passage in Jeremiah? Yes, the Lord is the Husband and Israel and Judah corporately together are His wife, but there is more, for the Lord said He will make a new covenant with His wife[51]. One in which will not be written on tablets of stone but written on hearts and minds. Ezekiel goes further and prophesies in Ezekiel 36:24-26 NKJV:

For I will take you from among the nations, gather you out of all countries, and bring you into your own land. Then I will sprinkle clean water on you, and you shall be clean; I will cleanse you from all your filthiness and from all your idols. I will give you a new heart and put a new spirit within you; I will take the heart of stone out of your flesh and give you a heart of flesh.

When we read Revelation 19:7 which says:

Let us be glad and rejoice and give Him glory, for the marriage of the Lamb has come, and His wife has made herself ready

then we must understand the legal document to legitimise this marriage of the Lamb, is the New Covenant which was promised to Israel long before Jesus was born. The two cannot be separated, but one is a fulfilment of the other:

---

[51] There is not a separate marriage between the Father and Israel, and between Jesus and the church, this is not correct! We quickly get into all manner of nonsense when we separate the two. Jesus came to inaugurate the new covenant promised by the Father to Israel centuries earlier. The new marriage covenant remains with Israel. It is only by virtue of being grafted into the Olive Tree (Israel) that the gentile church can enter the marriage covenant that already exists between the Lord and Israel.

The Marriage of the Lamb is a fulfilment of the promise made between the Lord and Israel.

When Jesus took the cup and declared in Matthew 26:28 *"this is my blood of the new covenant"* He was saying to His disciples who were with Him that night, *"through Me the New Covenant promised long before to your forefathers has come."* Yes, it is a New Covenant, but it has an ancient history! And though the *'Old is fading away and will soon disappear'* (Hebrews 8:13), its purpose of providing the basis of marriage between God and man continues in the New. It is only because the Gentiles have been grafted into the olive tree that is Israel[52], that they are able to participate in the promises made to Israel[53]. There can be no wedding without Israel, for there is but one Wife. No secret rapture of a gentile church to a wedding without the very one with whom the promises of a new covenant have been made, how can this be?[54] There is a spiritual law, as Paul writes:

First for the Jew, and then the Greek (or Gentile)[55].

This law not only applies to salvation and judgement but in marriage also. As Laban said to Jacob when Jacob realised he had been tricked into marrying Leah before Rachel:

"It is not our custom here," Laban replied, "to give the younger daughter in marriage before the firstborn." (Genesis 29:26 NET).

---

[52] Romans 11:17.

[53] Romans 9:4.

[54] On a personal note, I am always amazed by the popularity of adopting the ancient Jewish wedding customs to the Gentile church to support a pre-tribulation rapture view, or imminent/unexpected return of Jesus to take away His Bride. In this way almost akin to robbing Israel of what belongs to her and leaving her outside the wedding.

[55] Romans 1:16, 2:9.

QB20 What's the Difference Between a Wife and a Bride?

I can't speak for all the wedding customs around the world, but in the UK the marriage doesn't take place when a couple become engaged and betrothed to each other, but only upon completion of the legally accepted marriage ceremony, usually in a church or registry office. When people are engaged, they are not yet officially married, and their relationship is not yet legally binding. The marriage certificate is only produced once the wedding ceremony has been completed. During the wedding ritual, it is customary for the Bride to wear a wedding dress and if in a church, she will proceed to walk up the aisle to the altar, where she will stand alongside the man she is to marry, at which point the person officiating the wedding will lead the couple through their vows and legal declarations until the final statement is made: *"I now pronounce you husband and wife"*.

Leading up to her wedding day the betrothed woman is called the *'Bride to be'*, then on the actual day of the wedding she is *'the bride'*, and finally upon completion of the wedding ceremony, the Bride becomes the *'wife'*, and is thereafter known and called the wife of the husband. This is somewhat different to the Jewish wedding customs of Jesus' time. In a traditional Jewish wedding, the first stage of the marriage was the betrothal in which a contract (known as a *'ketubbah'*) was signed and legally binding. At this stage, the couple are considered to be fully married, although consummation is not yet permitted, and the wedding feast remains until after the consummation. Remember Mary and Joseph? The angel of the Lord appeared to Joseph in a dream and said:

don't be afraid to take Mary as your wife. (Matthew 1:20 NET).

They were betrothed; engaged to each other. And though their relationship had not yet been consummated, Mary was still Joseph's wife. Because the contract was legally binding, Joseph intended to divorce Mary privately to avoid her being disgraced (Matthew 1:18,19).

Now that we know it is the wife who becomes the Bride, and not the Bride that becomes the wife, let's look again at Revelation 19:7:

Let us be glad and rejoice, and give honour to him: for the marriage of the Lamb is come, and his wife has made herself ready.

Though some translations say: *'his Bride has made herself ready'*, a study of the Greek shows the word used here is *'gynē'* (goo-nay) meaning *'wife'*, and is the same word used when referring to Mary as the wife of Joseph. The word for *'Bride'* is *'nymphē'* (noom-fay) and is the word used in Revelation 21:2:

Then I, John, saw the holy city, the New Jerusalem, coming down out of heaven from God, prepared as a Bride adorned (beautifully dressed) for her husband.

Why is this distinction between a wife and a Bride important? What is the difference between the two? You see being a wife means that although there is a wedding contract in place which exists in the New Covenant, being a wife does not mean she is necessarily ready for her wedding day. Whereas being the Bride, means she has made herself or is at least making herself ready because she knows her Bridegroom is coming. For this, the Bride must be adorned and beautifully dressed for her husband as in Revelation 21. Being the Bride is about preparation[56], beautification[57], glorification[58] and consummation. Ephesians 5:31,32 [NKJV] reads:

For this reason a man shall leave his father and mother and be joined to his wife, and the two shall become one flesh. This is a great mystery, but I speak concerning Christ and the church.

Jesus our glorious Bridegroom King is coming for His wife that He might be one with her in a much more profound and intimate way than the way we understand being one and intimate with Him now. Yes, there is an intimacy shared which we have with Jesus now, but there is a Bridal intimacy much deeper anticipated. He paid the price for His wife two thousand years ago when He died for her as her Kinsman Redeemer. He was then, is now and ever shall be ready for her. What He waits for now, is for His wife to make herself ready for Him; for His wife to be His bride, beautifully dressed, adorned and glorious.

---

[56] Matthew 25:1-13 This is the parable of the ten virgins. See Quick Bite 3.
[57] that He might present her to Himself a glorious church, not having spot or wrinkle or any such thing, but that she should be holy and without blemish. (Ephesians 5:27 NKJV).
[58] For a man indeed ought not to cover his head, since he is the image and glory of God; but woman is the glory of man. (1 Corinthians 11:7 NKJV).

QB21 How Does the Wife Get Dressed?

L ast time we saw the difference between being a wife and a bride. A wife is the one with whom the wedding contract has been established, but it is the Bride who enters into the consummation of the marriage. Being a wife is not enough, just like being one of the ten virgins was not enough, for she must also prepare and be ready for when the Bridegroom returns. That means having oil in our lamps and wedding garments in which to be dressed.

> *Being the Bride is about adornment, about being beautiful and fully compatible for the Groom.*

John sees in Revelation 21:2 the New Jerusalem coming down out of Heaven like a bride beautifully dressed for her husband. So if the wife is to be dressed, how does she receive her wedding garments? Revelation 19:8 says:

And to her it was granted to be arrayed in fine linen, clean and bright, for the fine linen is the righteous acts of the saints.

This verse makes the connection between being and doing. Between what it means to be dressed like a bride and the actions taken by her. For the *'fine linen is the righteous acts of the saints.'* Being requires doing, for in the process of doing we become[59]. Paul makes this connection between who we are and the work required to grow very well when he writes to the Ephesians in 4:11-16 [NKJV]saying:

And He Himself gave some to be apostles, some prophets, some evangelists, and some pastors and teachers, for the equipping of the saints for the work of ministry, for the edifying of the body of Christ, till we all come to the unity of the faith and of the knowledge of the Son of God, to a perfect man, to the measure of the stature of the fullness of Christ; that we should no longer be children, tossed to and fro and carried about with every wind of doctrine, by the trickery of men, in the cunning craftiness of deceitful plotting, but, speaking the truth in love, may grow up in all things into Him who is the head--Christ-- from whom the whole body, joined and knit together by what every joint supplies, according to the effective working by which every part does its share, causes growth of the body for the edifying of itself in love.

There is a progression here in Paul's writing. First of all, we learn there have been gifts given which we know as the apostle, prophet, evangelist, pastor and teacher.

> *But when we look at this passage from a Bridal perspective, we realise these appointments are given by the Bridegroom so His Bride can get ready.*

---

[59] I am not suggesting here that we become the Wife by doing, but rather the necessity for preparation as the Bride requires more than a passive waiting but a pro-active determination to make oneself ready by 'righteous acts of the saints'.

She has to grow up into maturity. How will you know she is fully grown? Well, Paul gives the answer when he writes she will have a stature measured by the fulness of Christ. This happens when each part of the body is equipped to do the work of the ministry, and as each part does its work, so it builds itself up in love.

In answer to our question: How does the wife get dressed? The point I am making is that there are works for her to do, but more, in fact I believe there are bridal assignments that only she can fulfil, because it will take the church with a bridal mindset[60] and relationship with each other in oneness, to have bestowed upon her the anointing and authority necessary for the assignment to be achieved. How will we know or recognise if the Bride is getting dressed? Well, one sure way is how she will take a resemblance to her Bridegroom more and more. In fact, Jesus Himself said to His disciples on their last supper together in John 14:12-14[NKJV]:

12 Most assuredly, I say to you, he who believes in Me, the works that I do he will do also; and greater works than these he will do, because I go to My Father. 13 And whatever you ask in My name, that I will do, that the Father may be glorified in the Son. 14 If you ask anything in My name, I will do it.

---

[60] I call this 'Bridal consciousness'. If we understand the office of Apostle, Prophet, Evangelist, Pastor, and Teacher are gifts given by the Bridegroom, then it is vital those called into these leadership roles should have a bridal mindset.

QB22 How Should I Approach the Book of Revelation?

The opening of the Book of Revelation reads:

> The Revelation of Jesus Christ, which God gave him, to show his servants things which must shortly come to pass; and he sent and signified it by his angel to his servant John: Who bore record of the word of God, and of the testimony of Jesus Christ, and of all things that he saw. (Revelation 1:1,2).

Right from the outset we are given the foundational truth and purpose for this last book of the Bible, and it begins by saying *The Revelation of Jesus Christ'*. This word *'revelation'* in the ancient Greek is *'apokalypsis'* which simply means *'to make known something that was previously unknown, to reveal something hidden, a laying bare, making naked, to disclose the truth about someone, an unveiling'*. What is it this book is to unveil? It is the unveiling of Jesus, it is to make Him fully known, not only in the words of this prophecy but in the literal sense - when the events which this prophecy foretell actually take place. At that time, the whole world will see who Jesus truly is, for He will be on full display to consummate the Kingdom of God upon the Earth and to be joined to His wife forever Ephesians 5:31. This end-time prophecy is all about His unveiling, the revelation of Jesus Christ. But more than His unveiling, He is also the One bringing the revelation, as verse 1 says it is *'Revelation of Jesus Christ which God gave Him'*. Not given, as in Jesus saw something that He didn't see before, for as fully God, Jesus is omniscient, all-knowing with the Father. No, it was given to Jesus to make the revelation of Himself, for He was worthy to take the scroll and to open its seals.

This is so important for us to understand and apply whenever we read this most profound last book of the Bible. For though the record contains all manner of visions and encounters which John had, the ultimate purpose of this book is to glorify and magnify the Lord Jesus Christ. After we have speculated and debated on such glimpses of the seals, trumpets and bowls, the antichrist and false prophet, the fall of Mystery Babylon, the Second Coming, the Millennium and the New Jerusalem, let us ensure we are not overly distracted by such things in a way that leads us down a path which does not have Jesus in full view.

> *For this is His Revelation, its purpose is to put Him at the centre and make known to us the full nature of who He is and what He will accomplish in the days to follow.*

Ultimately there is nothing gained and much to lose if we approach this most wonderful book of Revelation from mere curiosity and intellectualism. For it is not an appeal to the mind so much as it is to the heart, to the spirit of man, to quicken not our rational thought but our spiritual alertness, so we might align ourselves to who He is and what will shortly take place.

> *The correct response to this prophecy or any prophecy is to worship God because in His sovereign grace He is permitting us to see into matters concerning the future that we might know Him now.*

So, in answer to our question: *'How should I approach the book of Revelation?'* we should do so in pursuit of knowing Jesus more, for ultimately, He is the one speaking to us through this prophecy. This is the Revelation of Jesus, though He has sent His angel to testify, it is His testimony.

Then I fell down at his feet to worship him, but he said to me, "You must not do that! I am a fellow servant with you and your brothers who hold to the testimony of Jesus. Worship God." For the testimony of Jesus is the spirit of prophecy. (Revelation 19:10 ESV).

QB23 The Testimony of Jesus is the Spirit of Prophecy (Part 1)

T he Book of Revelation begins with these words:

> The Revelation of Jesus Christ, which God gave him, to show his servants things which must shortly come to pass; and he sent and signified it by his angel to his servant John: who bore record of the word of God, and of the testimony of Jesus Christ, and of all things that he saw. (Revelation 1:1,2).

The underlying purpose of Revelation is to reveal Jesus, to make Him known now and to signify how His glory will be revealed to the whole world in the coming days. This is what these opening verses in Revelation tell us - that God gave to Jesus to show His Revelation to His servants things which must shortly come to pass. The phrase *'things which must shortly come to pass'*, positions this prophecy into the future. It is what we might call *'predictive'* prophecy and not *'historical'*. Most scholars agree Revelation was written around 96AD whilst John was exiled on Patmos, and therefore we might reasonably ascribe much of what is written after this date. As we learnt in Quick Bite 13, *'shortly'* doesn't mean imminent or at any time, but quickly, when the things John sees taking place occur, they will do so quickly.

The opening continues and shows the means by which our Lord would signify and attest to His revelation is by sending His angel to

John. The angels are Jesus' servants, communicating His revelation to John. And throughout this prophecy we see many angels involved in the administration of these signs and visions for John to witness, which he wrote down as instructed[61]. So what we have in Revelation is the written record of what John saw, and our pages are filled with strange visions like a seven-headed beast with ten horns coming out of the sea[62], or a city coming out of heaven dressed like a bride[63]. John, no doubt, found the same challenge as did Paul who saw things too sacred to be put into the limitation of human language[64]. But a vision inspires the imagination and gives room for the Holy Spirit to enlighten. So as John witnessed and recorded the Revelation of Jesus Christ, he encountered many angels with various roles and assignments, which we find punctuating the unfolding of the prophetic narrative, but in particular, and as indicated here in

---

[61] Write the things which you have seen, and the things which are, and the things which will take place after this. (Revelation 1:19 NKJV).

[62] Then I stood on the sand of the sea. And I saw a beast rising up out of the sea, having seven heads and ten horns, and on his horns ten crowns, and on his heads a blasphemous name. Now the beast which I saw was like a leopard, his feet were like the feet of a bear, and his mouth like the mouth of a lion. The dragon gave him his power, his throne, and great authority. And I saw one of his heads as if it had been mortally wounded, and his deadly wound was healed. And all the world marvelled and followed the beast. So they worshipped the dragon who gave authority to the beast; and they worshipped the beast, saying, "Who is like the beast? Who is able to make war with him?" (Revelation 13:1-4 NKJV).

[63] Then I, John, saw the holy city, New Jerusalem, coming down out of heaven from God, prepared as a bride adorned for her husband. (Revelation 21:2 NKJV).

[64] I know a man in Christ who fourteen years ago--whether in the body I do not know, or whether out of the body I do not know, God knows-- such a one was caught up to the third heaven. And I know such a man-- whether in the body or out of the body I do not know, God knows-- how he was caught up into Paradise and heard inexpressible words, which it is not lawful for a man to utter. (2 Corinthians 12:2-4 NKJV).

Revelation 1:1 there is one angel in particular commission by Jesus who sent His angel to John, to testify on His behalf. Chapter 22:16 also supports this and reads:

I, Jesus, have sent My angel to testify to you these things in the churches. I am the Root and the Offspring of David, the Bright and Morning Star.

The word I want to point out here is the word *'testify'*, Jesus sent His angel to testify. In other words, the revelation of Jesus is given to us in the form of testimony, His testimony. This is what our opening verses in chapter 1 tell us, for it says that John *'bore record of the word of God, and of the testimony of Jesus Christ, and of all things that he saw'*. The revelation of Jesus comes to us as *'The testimony of Jesus'*, and in Revelation 19:10 the angel informs John, that:

the testimony of Jesus is the Spirit of Prophecy.

In summary, the point I am making is the revelation of Jesus, that which He is revealing to us about himself and about the things to come, it comes to us in the form of His testimony, *'the testimony of Jesus'*. And when Jesus testifies, His words are carried by His messengers, in this case His angel, but in all cases and ultimately by the Holy Spirit who is *'the Spirit of Prophecy'*. The testimony of Jesus is prophetic because it is revelatory.

QB24 The Testimony of Jesus is the Spirit of Prophecy (Part 2)

L ast time I made the point the Revelation of Jesus comes to us in the form of a testimony, His testimony, *'the testimony of Jesus'*. Though messengers, like His angel, may testify on His behalf, it still remains His testimony. Ultimately the testimony of Jesus, whether carried by men or angels, are enabled to do so through the Holy Spirit, which is also called the *'Spirit of Prophecy'*.

The word *'testimony'* in ancient Greek is *'martyria' (mar-too-ree'-ah)* and is described as the responsibility committed to the prophets to testify concerning future events. But the word *'testimony'* also has a legal connotation, meaning *'one who testifies before a judge or gives testimony in a court of law'*. When looking at the testimony of Jesus from a legal perspective, we catch a glimpse into the courts of Heaven and the protocol being enacted. The testimony of Jesus bears witness in the heavenly courts, of all that He is, all that He has accomplished and all that He is entitled to. For example, in nullifying the legal certificates and decrees against us, Colossians 2:13-15[NET] reads:

And even though you were dead in your transgressions and in the uncircumcision of your flesh, he nevertheless made you alive with him, having forgiven all your transgressions. He has destroyed what was against us, a certificate of indebtedness expressed in decrees opposed to us. He has taken it away by nailing it to the cross. Disarming the rulers and authorities, he has made a public disgrace of them, triumphing over them by the cross.

Jesus' testimony endures in the heavenly courts and testifies in our defence against the rulers and authorities, disarming their claims of outstanding debt, because the testimony of Jesus declares that the ransom for us has been paid in full, and the righteous requirements of the law have been met because He is the Lamb who was slain. In Revelation 5[NKJV] we see this courtroom in session. The chapter begins:

And I saw in the right hand of Him who sat on the throne a scroll written inside and on the back, sealed with seven seals. Then I saw a strong angel proclaiming with a loud voice, "Who is worthy to open the scroll and to loose its seals?"

We read there was no one worthy found anywhere, except the Lion of the tribe of Judah, and John sees the Lion as a Lamb, who comes and takes the scroll out of the right hand of Him who is sat on the throne. Jesus was able to take the scroll because of who He is, His testimony makes Him worthy.

And they sang a new song, saying: "You are worthy to take the scroll, And to open its seals; For You were slain, And have redeemed us to God by Your blood Out of every tribe and tongue and people and nation, And have made us kings and priests to our God; And we shall reign on the earth." (Revelation 5:9-10 NKJV).

The testimony of Jesus not only reveals things to come but is also used in a judicial sense. His testimony is of the highest honour, and cannot be refuted by any power of hell. His testimony gives the legal right to enforce and transact the Eternal Purpose of God. Now the testimony of Jesus is part of who He is and is embedded in His wonderful name. His name is higher than any other and is supported by His testimony, so that when we pray *'in the name of Jesus'* we are calling upon His testimony as in a court of law, which gives absolute authority and permission granted for the matter to proceed in our favour. When contemplating the name of Jesus, John Newton who wrote the hymn Amazing Grace also penned these words:

How sweet the name of Jesus sounds in a believer's ear! It soothes our sorrows, heals our wounds and drives away our fear.

It makes the wounded spirit whole and calms the troubled breast; 'tis manna to the hungry soul, and to the weary, rest.

O Jesus, shepherd, guardian, friend, my Prophet, Priest, and King, my Lord, my Life, my Way, my End, accept the praise I bring.

How weak the effort of my heart, how cold my warmest thought; but when I see you as you are, I'll praise you as I ought.

Till then I would your love proclaim with every fleeting breath; and may the music of your name refresh my soul in death.

QB25 The Testimony of Jesus is the Spirit of Prophecy (Part 3)

As the world moves towards the finality of this dispensation there is an acceleration of wickedness upon the earth. Satanic forces are manoeuvring and implementing their dark plans, which are unfolding in both the visible and invisible realms. The Bride must not be blind or unable to see the reality of what's really going on around her. She must be aware of the battle being played out and the nature of the warfare in which she is engaged. For she is not called to be a spectator. Neither is she an overcomer only, but she is called to be a warrior Bride and prophetess, to participate in the will and purpose of God in the last days. What will be the hallmark of the end-time warrior bride? Well, scripture gives us a great window into the future to see her qualities:

And they overcame him by the blood of the lamb, and by the word of their testimony, and they did not love their lives to the death. (Revelation 12:11).

This well-known verse specifically mentions three qualities describing the end-time warrior bride. Firstly, they overcome Satan by the blood of the Lamb! Hallelujah! The context of this verse is that Satan – the accuser, has been hurled down to the earth to accuse the brethren before God day and night. But by the blood, and only by the blood are our sins atoned for, and any accusation from Satan is answered most powerfully by the blood which has paid the debt in full[65] and washed the sin away[66]. The blood of Jesus will never lose its power and speaks continually on our behalf[67] in the same courtroom that Satan brings his accusations. Another quality of the overcomers listed in this verse is how they loved not their life even unto death. Jesus is their Lord, and their commitment to Him is total. They love Him more than they love life itself, and if the price for obedience and loyalty is their death, then their faith knows there is glory which awaits them beyond death's veil, for death has lost its sting and serves only as the doorway through which they will pass into immortality.

Now there is one other quality mentioned in Revelation 12:11 which says they overcome Satan *by 'the word of their testimony'*. We usually understand this as the story of our salvation, indeed when asked to give our testimony, that's usually what we mean. But I believe there is more here we can glean from this phrase *'the word of their testimony'*. Let's read what John writes later in this chapter:

Then the dragon became furious with the woman and went off to make war on the rest of her offspring, on those who keep the commandments of God and hold to the testimony of

---

[65] knowing that you were not redeemed with corruptible things, like silver or gold, from your aimless conduct received by tradition from your fathers, but with the precious blood of Christ, as of a lamb without blemish and without spot. (1 Peter 1:18.19 NKJV).

[66] But if we walk in the light as He is in the light, we have fellowship with one another, and the blood of Jesus Christ His Son cleanses us from all sin. (1 John 1:7 NKJV).

[67] to Jesus the Mediator of the new covenant, and to the blood of sprinkling that speaks better things than that of Abel. (Hebrews 12:24 NKJV).

Jesus. And he stood on the sand of the sea. (Revelation 12:17 ESV).

There is a connection here between verse 11 and verse 17, between the *'word of their testimony'* and *'the testimony of Jesus'.* Whilst I am not saying the word of their testimony is not the story of their salvation, I am suggesting it is more than this, and that

> **the word of their testimony is the testimony of Jesus.**

There is precedent for this both with angels and man. Remember in Revelation 22:16 Jesus said:

I have sent my angel to testify to you these things.

You could say the word of the angel's testimony was the testimony of Jesus. In Revelation 1:9 John records he:

Was on the island that is called Patmos for the word of God and for the testimony of Jesus Christ.

John's testimony was the testimony of Jesus. In the same way, we have been given the Testimony of Jesus through which we can overcome our adversary. Remember the word *'testimony'* has a legal connotation, as someone's testimony before a judge or court of law, this is what we have been entrusted with; the Testimony of Jesus in which we can stand. A position of justification and redemption, yes, which is our defence, but the Testimony of Jesus is also our offence; the means to advance and to enforce legal jurisdiction. When we pray *'in the name of Jesus'* it is because the name of Jesus is supported by His testimony as in a court of law, and when His name is used and therefore His testimony invoked it gives the legal right for the matter to proceed in our favour.

QB26 The Testimony of Jesus is the Spirit of Prophecy (Part 4)

In studying the *'testimony of Jesus'*, so far we have seen the meaning of testimony in a legal context because the ancient Greek word *'martyria'* (*mar-too-ree'-ah*) has a legal connotation as *'one who testifies before a judge or gives testimony in a court of law'* but the word *'martyria'* is also described as *'the responsibility committed to the prophets to testify concerning future events.'* The Revelation of Jesus comes to us as the Testimony of Jesus, but also the Lord appoints others to testify His revelation on His behalf, just like His angel in Revelation 22:16, and here also in our key text Revelation 19:10 [ESV]:

Then I (that is John) fell down at his feet (the angel) to worship him, but he said to me, "You must not do that! I am a fellow servant with you and your brothers who hold to the testimony of Jesus. Worship God. For the testimony of Jesus is the spirit of prophecy."

The angel was testifying on the Lord's behalf and was telling John, don't worship me, I'm a fellow servant with you, what I have been revealing to you is not my testimony but the Testimony of Jesus, therefore worship Him, because the *'Testimony of Jesus is the Spirit of Prophecy'*. When talking of testimony here, I am referring to the prophetic definition of testifying about future events. In this context, the testimony of Jesus is the revealing by Jesus of things to come, but it comes to us, as it did the angel, by the Spirit of Prophecy. This is what Jesus said when speaking of the Holy Spirit in John 16:12-15[NKJV]:

I still have many things to say to you, but you cannot bear them now. However, when He, the Spirit of truth, has come, He will guide you into all truth; for He will not speak on His own authority, but whatever He hears He will speak; and He will tell you things to come. He will glorify Me, for He will take of what is Mine and declare to you. All things that the Father has are Mine. Therefore I said that He will take of Mine and declare it to you.

Jesus revealed there was still much he wanted to tell his disciples, but He was not able because they could not bear any more at that time. Indeed, we know after His resurrection, Jesus spent forty days teaching them many things about the Kingdom[68]. But the instruction here is He would speak to them through the Holy Spirit specifically about the *'things to come'*. So this doesn't refer to His teaching before His ascension, for at that time they had not yet been baptised in the Holy Spirit. The Holy Spirit will come. And when He comes '*He will not speak on his own authority*', but the testimony of Jesus about the things to come. The apostle Peter also taught on this same principle when he writes in 1 Peter 1:10-11[HCSB]:

Concerning this salvation, the prophets who prophesied about the grace that would come to you searched and carefully investigated. They inquired into what time or what circumstances the Spirit of Christ within them was indicating when He (that is the Holy Spirit) testified in

---

[68] Acts 1:3.

advance to the messianic sufferings and the glories that would follow.

Peter teaches it was the Spirit of Christ within the prophets who testified in advance of the things to come, not only the work of the Cross but also the glories that would follow. This is the Spirit of Prophecy at work, empowering and activating the Testimony of Jesus within his servants. Remember the end-time saints will '*hold to the testimony of Jesus*', I believe this means they will hold to the '*spirit of prophecy*'. There will be an outpouring of the Holy Spirit, the '*Spirit of Prophecy*' to empower the church to rise up as a warrior Bride, a prophetess, who will have the testimony of Jesus upon her lips, to make prophetic declaration upon the earth of matters being legislated in the Heavens. For there the Lamb has taken the scroll and will open its seals as the administration of the apocalypse unfolds. A unification between Heaven and Earth, as the Bride begins her final preparations not only to be dressed in fine linen, but to be His glory upon the earth, learning to reign with Him in the closing hours of this era, and going before Him in the Spirit of Elijah, like John the Baptist to make His paths straight.

QB27 The Testimony of Jesus is the Spirit of Prophecy (Part 5)

I n concluding this mini-series, I'd like to summarise, if possible, the last four parts into this one statement:

> *The Spirit of Prophecy activates the testimony of Jesus within His servants, so that they may testify on His behalf. This testimony of Jesus has legal right and authority in the courts of Heaven and is invoked whenever we pray in the name of Jesus, so that, first, we are able to overcome Satan our adversary, and secondly, we can enforce matters legislated upon in the Heavenly courts. The Spirit of Prophecy brings the revelation of Jesus to us that we might know the things shortly to take place.*

Just as with His disciples, there are things Jesus wants to say to us about what is to come, and He will send the Spirit of Prophecy to speak on His behalf. This process of receiving revelation is not purely contained with the scriptures but is being spoken by the Spirit even now because revelation is developmental, and as one draws closer to the event in view, so the details become clearer. There is a principle scholars call '*prophetic foreshortening*' which is similar to what happens when we view a landscape from far away, when we are far away it is difficult to differentiate distances between objects that are close together. The biblical prophecies are all authentic and without error, yet the prophets of old saw things from afar[69], but as the day draws nearer, we are in a position to see the details more clearly because we are much closer. For example, how could anyone of John's time, or older yet, in Isaiah's time, comprehend the technological age we are now in? Even so, we desperately need and are so grateful for the prophetic record given to us in scripture. These form the very platform, the vantage point upon which we stand as we gaze further into the coming unveiling. Now here is an important principle that must be observed in dealing with prophecy – never remove the foundation!

> *All prophecy in the Word of God is foundational. Even though we accept the Spirit of Prophecy is still speaking today, it will always be consistent and serve to bring further revelation on what has already been written.*

That's why we must know the Word, because in the last days there will be many false prophets, and we must be able to recognise the counterfeit by knowing the truth. There is much being spoken today which is neither consistent with the Word of God, nor the ways of God. How will you know the difference? By developing a sensitivity to the inner voice of the Holy Spirit which comes from a lifestyle of personal study in the Word, and a daily walk of intimacy with the Lord. Amos 3:7 reads:

---

[69] These all died in faith, not having received the promises, but having seen them afar off were assured of them, embraced them and confessed that they were strangers and pilgrims on the earth. (Hebrews 11:13 NKJV) "for assuredly, I say to you that many prophets and righteous men desired to see what you see, and did not see [it], and to hear what you hear, and did not hear it. (Matthew 13:17 NKJV)

Surely the Lord GOD does nothing, unless He reveals His secret to His servants the prophets.

The word secret is *'cowd' (sode)* and means *'secret counsel, intimacy with God, an assembly'*. The Septuagint puts it like this:

For in no way shall the Lord God do a thing that he should not uncover (or reveal) instruction to his servants the prophets.

Instruction here means to tutor, educate or train, to nurture. Beloved, we are in training! We are being led into greater depths of intimacy, nurtured and trained to be able to discern the secrets of the Lord ahead of time.

> *It is time for the Bride to arise and to take on the prophet's mantle, for there are things which the Lord Jesus himself will declare as His testimony in the Heavenly Court, which will be a prophecy in the heart and upon the lips of His end-time warrior bride.*

This is so important; we must take responsibility and act now. For without maturity, we are not equipped for the days ahead. The Bride bridges heaven and earth. She is seated with her Bridegroom in heavenly places, but she is also planted on the land as a warrior and a prophetess in the Spirit of Elijah, like John the Baptist, to prepare the way of the Lord. The Bride must awake with a revived spiritual perception, a new lens, a new paradigm, a new prophetic consciousness.

QB28 The Warrior Returns

Then I saw heaven opened, and behold, a white horse! The one sitting on it is called Faithful and True, and in righteousness he judges and makes war. (Revelation 19:11 ESV).

Once the marriage of the Lamb has come, (because His wife has made herself ready,) the first thing John sees is a rider on a white horse. Some draw a similarity here with the rider in Revelation 6:2[NET]:

So I looked, and here came a white horse! The one who rode it had a bow, and he was given a crown, and as a conqueror he rode out to conquer.

On that occasion, the white horse appears upon the opening of the first seal, and no other explicit mention is given of the horse or its rider for the rest of Revelation. It is hard to reconcile these two riders as being the same because of the numerous differences between them. The first rider has no name, whereas the rider in Revelation 19 is ascribed several names:

- Faithful and True v11,

- the Word of God v13[70], and

---

[70] He was clothed with a robe dipped in blood, and His name is called The Word of God. (Revelation 19:13 NKJV).

- King of Kings and Lord of Lords[71] v16

which unmistakably identifies Him as our Lord Jesus Christ. The first rider had a bow, whereas Jesus has a sharp sword which comes out of His mouth[72]. The unnamed rider was given a crown whereas Jesus is crowned with many crowns[73]. The unnamed rider is actually one of four horsemen who are connected with the opening of the first four seals, whereas Jesus is the One who opens the seals[74]. What does connect them, is they are both conquerors, although their fates are very different. The first horseman we'll come back to another time, so now let's put Jesus in full view.

The vision John saw in Revelation 19 was a clear picture of Christ returning as a warrior. On Jesus first coming He rode into Jerusalem on a donkey which is a symbol of peace, but on His second coming He will return on a white horse a symbol of war. Our opening verse 11 of chapter 19 says in righteousness Jesus will *'judge and make war'*, we might ask who will Jesus make war with? Well in Revelation 16:14 we see the kings of the world being gathered together in Armageddon *'for the battle of the great day of God Almighty'* and in

---

[71] And He has on His robe and on His thigh a name written: KING OF KINGS AND LORD OF LORDS. (Revelation 19:16).

[72] Now out of His mouth goes a sharp sword, that with it He should strike the nations. And He Himself will rule them with a rod of iron. He Himself treads the winepress of the fierceness and wrath of Almighty God. (Revelation 19:15).

[73] His eyes were like a flame of fire, and on His head were many crowns. He had a name written that no one knew except Himself. (Revelation 19:12).

[74] Now I saw when the Lamb opened one of the seals; and I heard one of the four living creatures saying with a voice like thunder, "Come and see." And I looked, and behold, a white horse. He who sat on it had a bow; and a crown was given to him, and he went out conquering and to conquer. (Revelation 6:1,2).

Revelation 17:14 there are ten kings described who go to make war with the Lamb[75]. There are also many other prophecies which forewarn the surrounding of Jerusalem by the nations of the world[76]. In addition to these armies and kings, this same term *'make war'* is found previously in Revelation 13:4:

So they worshipped the dragon who gave authority to the beast; and they worshipped the beast, saying, "Who is like the beast? Who is able to make war with him?"

The answer to that question will be answered by Jesus the warrior King! Jesus will make war with the beast and with the false prophet.

Then the beast was captured, and with him the false prophet who worked signs in his presence, by which he deceived those who received the mark of the beast and those who worshipped his image. These two were cast alive into the lake of fire burning with brimstone. (Revelation 19:20).

This is an important point to secure in our understanding lest we be fooled into thinking of some other alternative. It is Jesus Christ who defeats the beast and the false prophet, not vicariously through the church, but by His actual physical return. The demise of these two enemies of God happens after Jesus returns and not before. The passage is quite clear on this point, which then makes it very difficult

---

[75] The ten horns which you saw are ten kings who have received no kingdom as yet, but they receive authority for one hour as kings with the beast.

These are of one mind, and they will give their power and authority to the beast.

These will make war with the Lamb, and the Lamb will overcome them, for He is Lord of lords and King of kings; and those who are with Him are called, chosen, and faithful. (Revelation 17:12-14).

[76] Zechariah 12:3, 14:2, Micah 4:11-13.

to hold to a victorious church, post-millennial viewpoint, without allegorising this text. What I'm saying is the plain sense meaning of the passage states the Beast and False Prophet are only captured and thrown alive in the lake of fire after Jesus returns. This means for the notion of a victorious church era and Kingdom Now doctrine - something has to be done with this passage because it is hard to reconcile a euphoric millennial age until the Beast and False Prophet have been eliminated.

This one truth forms the very foundation of our hope, that Jesus Christ is coming back, and when He comes, He will come as a warrior, as King of Kings and Lord and Lords to make war against our enemies and His. He will be crowned with many crowns and will reign forever and ever in righteousness and justice. Let us therefore set our hopes on His glorious return more than on our successes, more than on whatever advantage we think we have now, for His glory shall be ours also. What is it we have now, that will compare to what we shall have then? What state might we achieve now, to that which shall be then? No, let us fix our eyes on Jesus the author and perfecter of our faith, not only for the Saviour that He is but also as the Warrior Bridegroom King who is coming to reign!

QB29 The Armies in Heaven

When Jesus returns as the warrior, to judge and make war in Revelation 19:11 He will not be coming alone.

And the armies in heaven, clothed in fine linen, white and clean, followed Him on white horses. (Revelation 19:14).

This naturally raises the question: Who are these clothed in fine linen white and clean following Jesus? For whoever they are, the Bible says they are already in heaven before the Lord's return to make war. Otherwise, it would not be possible for an army to follow the Lord who comes out of heaven if the army were not already in heaven also. The text describes this army as being clothed in fine linen white and clean, this is very similar to the description of the wedding garments, although there is a difference in the word used for white. The white clothing of the army is the word *'leukos'* (*loo k-ah-s*), meaning *'dazzling light, brightness, like the garments of angels, and of those exalted to the splendour of the heavenly state'*. It symbolises a glorified form. The word *'leukos'* also means *'shining or white garments worn on festive or state occasions and of white garments as the sign of innocence and purity of the soul'*. *'Leukos'* is the word used when describing the transfiguration of Jesus:

and He was transfigured before them. His face shone like the sun, and His clothes became as white as the light. (Matthew 17:2).

The word white(bright) used for the wedding garments[77] is not *'leukos'* as it was for the armies but is the word *'lampros'* (lam-pras) meaning *'brilliant, clear, splendid and magnificent, elegance in dress or style'*. Truly these are the wedding garments, she will be clothed magnificently, elegant, shining and brilliant. The two descriptions are very similar but have a slightly different emphasis.

Okay, what we know so far about these armies is

1) They are already in Heaven because that's what the verse says, they are in heaven and they follow the Lord who comes out of Heaven, and

2) They are wearing fine linen, white and clean.

Now to me, there are only two possible answers of who these riders on white horses could be: Either they are the Bride, or they are the angels. Maybe since verse 11 actually uses the plural *'armies'* it is both! Well, let's look at Revelation 17:14 to help further in the identification process.

They will make war with the Lamb, but the Lamb will conquer them, because he is Lord of lords and King of kings, and those accompanying the Lamb are the called, chosen, and faithful.

This helps to identify the company of those returning with the Lord as *'the called, chosen, and faithful'*. Because these terms are not used for angels, but for those who have been saved and remained faithful, we now know those who return as an army upon white horses following

---

[77] "Let us be glad and rejoice and give Him glory, for the marriage of the Lamb has come, and His wife has made herself ready." And to her it was granted to be arrayed in fine linen, clean and bright, for the fine linen is the righteous acts of the saints. (Revelation 19:7,8).

the Lord as He comes out of Heaven to make war, are His Bride! This is consistent with the context of the preceding passage of the Bride ready and arrayed in bright clean linen.

Does this mean the angels are not also returning? Indeed, the angels are also described as wearing pure and white linen Revelation 15:6[78]. Well, there are other passages that mention the angels returning with the Lord at various times like Matthew 13:41[79] talking of the end-time harvest, Matthew 24:31[80] a reference to the gathering of the elect after the tribulation and Matthew 25:31[81]. So in answer to our question: who are these returning with the Lord in Revelation 19? We can be confident it is a reference to the Bride, but because the term is plural, armies, and the angels are mentioned at various times in other passages specifically as returning with the Lord, it is reasonable to expect the angels will be among the Lord's armies when He returns. Why is this important? Because it helps to unravel

---

[78] And out of the temple came the seven angels having the seven plagues, clothed in pure bright linen, and having their chests girded with golden bands. (Revelation 15:6 NKJV).

[79] The Son of man shall send forth his angels, and they shall gather out of his kingdom all things that offend, and them which do iniquity; (Matthew 13:41 KJV).

[80] And he shall send his angels with a great sound of a trumpet, and they shall gather together his elect from the four winds, from one end of heaven to the other. (Matthew 24:31 KJV).

[81] When the Son of man shall come in his glory, and all the holy angels with him, then shall he sit upon the throne of his glory: (Matthew 25:31 KJV).

Whenever we read prophetic verses like these it is important not to assume that the events foretold necessarily follow each other immediately. That may indeed be the case, but there are many prophetic passages which string together future events in a couple of verses but are spaced out by a significant amount of time.

the chronology and sequence of future events which is necessary if we are to be prepared as we should for what lies ahead.

> *We cannot look at the Lord's return as a warrior in Revelation 19, as being the same time as the rapture, because this is the Bride returning with Her Bridegroom having already prepared, not the Bridegroom coming for His Bride.*

She is following the Lord out of Heaven, which means at this point she is not on the earth. Therefore, the rapture event takes place before this, and we'll come to that next time.

QB30 Unravelling the Rapture (Part 1)

I n taking a step-by-step approach in this Quick Bites series, I purposely started at the end of Revelation, because I wanted to put the Bride in full view from the outset. The Bride is the key to unlock the understanding of future events because this is the ultimate and Eternal Purpose of God. It is what He is after, His objective, His heart; to create an exquisite Bride for His Son. Having a Bridal consciousness enables us to see things from God's perspective, from a higher elevation, just like the angel in Revelation 21:9,10 who carried John in the Spirit to a great and high mountain to show him the Bride, the wife of the Lamb. When we take this higher elevation, we see things from a different lens, and once our eyes have been opened, we see the footprints of the Bride from Genesis 1 to Revelation 22.

Following on from last time, we have established when Jesus returns to judge and make war in Revelation 19, the Bride will be dressed and following behind.

> *Jesus isn't returning to earth for His Bride, He's returning to earth with His Bride.*

This leaves us with the question about the rapture, because if the Bride is in Heaven in Revelation 19, then that means she has been gathered up beforehand. The moment we talk of the rapture we are instantly into deep water, not least because the Bible never actually uses this word. Great care is needed in our exegesis if we are to navigate our way through the minefield of historic differences of opinion on the use of the word and when (or even if) it takes place.

The New Testament was originally written in Greek, and the word '*rapture*' is derived from the Latin translation of the Greek word '*harpazo*' (*har-pad'-zo*) which is in the Bible, meaning '*to seize, carry off by force, catch up, snatch out or away, pluck and pull*'. Though this word has lots of uses, and not necessarily in the way we are more familiar with, for clarity when mentioning the word '*rapture*', I am referring to the Greek word '*harpazo*' in the way Paul did, to mean a '*catching up in the clouds*' in 1 Thessalonians 4:17:

Then we who are alive and remain shall be caught up (harpazo, raptured) together with them in the clouds to meet the Lord in the air. And thus, we shall always be with the Lord.

The next challenge we face is that one of the most well know passages some people use to refer to the rapture actually doesn't use the word '*harpazo*' (rapture) at all.

Immediately after the tribulation of those days the sun will be darkened, and the moon will not give its light, and the stars will fall from heaven, and the powers of the heavens will be shaken. Then will appear in heaven the sign of the Son of Man, and then all the tribes of the earth will mourn, and they will see the Son of Man coming on the clouds of heaven with power and great glory. And he will send out his angels with a loud trumpet call, and they will gather his elect from the four winds, from one end of heaven to the other. (Matthew 24:29-31).

Jesus is teaching here, explaining He will send out His angels to gather His elect from one end of heaven to the other. The word to *'gather'* is *'episynágō'* (*ep-ee-soon-ag'-o*) meaning *'to gather together in one place, to bring together to others already assembled'*. There is nothing within the word itself to give any thought of gathering upwards into the air. This passage on its own would not be enough to support the rapture as we know it, because there's nothing to say those the angels gathered do not remain upon the earth. Indeed, the pre-tribulation[82] view is that this passage does not refer to the rapture, but as the physical gathering of the Jews back to Israel, which does happen of course, but I will share later how I see that unfolding. Next time, we will look a little more at Matthew 24 and other related passages to see if we can piece together a clearer picture, of the timing of the rapture. I want to give reasons why I don't just see this gathering relating to the physical return of the Jews to Israel[83] (as in the pre-tribulation view), and why I do see this gathering as the rapture described by Paul after the Tribulation.

---

[82] Viz, there is a rapture of the saints before the tribulation.

[83] I do not mean to suggest that the Jews will not be gathered to Israel, but as we shall see later, these particular verses in Mattew 24 are part of a wider picture of what is happening amongst both Jew and Gentile right at the end of the Great Tribulation.

QB31 Unravelling the Rapture (Part 2)

When considering the triumphant return of Jesus in Revelation 19; when He comes as King of Kings and Lord of Lords to judge and make war, I have already shared how at this stage the Bride is in Heaven, which necessitates an earlier rapture. This is a key point of the Bridal Perspective on the end times. Remember we must keep the Bride in full view because that's our blueprint to help us piece together the various pieces of the jigsaw. I believe the return of Jesus in Revelation 19 is not the same event as the coming of Jesus on the clouds in Matthew 24. To help bed this down a little further, that Revelation 19 is not synonymous with the gathering, I want to make some comparisons between the Warrior return in Revelation 19 and the gathering of the Elect in Matthew 24. So here are the two passages:

Then the sign of the Son of Man will appear in heaven, and all the tribes of the earth will mourn, and they will see the Son of Man coming on the clouds of heaven with power and great glory. And He will send His angels with a great sound of a trumpet, and they will gather together His elect from the four winds, from one end of heaven to the other. (Matthew 24:30,31).

11 Now I saw heaven opened, and behold, a white horse. And He who sat on him was called Faithful and True, and in righteousness He judges and makes war. 12 His eyes were

like a flame of fire, and on His head were many crowns. He had a name written that no one knew except Himself. 13 He was clothed with a robe dipped in blood, and His name is called The Word of God. 14 And the armies in heaven, clothed in fine linen, white and clean, followed Him on white horses. 15 Now out of His mouth goes a sharp sword, that with it He should strike the nations. And He Himself will rule them with a rod of iron. He Himself treads the winepress of the fierceness and wrath of Almighty God. 16 And He has on His robe and on His thigh a name written: KING OF KINGS AND LORD OF LORDS. (Revelation 19:11-16).

On closer study of these two passages, there are some very noticeable differences:

1. In Matthew, Jesus is coming on the clouds, whereas in Revelation, He is coming on a white horse

2. In Matthew, Jesus is coming with angels to gather the elect, whereas in Revelation, He is followed by His armies (who include the elect[84], His Bride) to make war

3. In Matthew, Jesus is named the Son of Man, whereas in Revelation, He is named Faithful and True, The Word of God and the King of Kings and Lord of Lords

4. In Matthew, Jesus has no weapon described, whereas in Revelation, He has a sharp sword coming out of His mouth

5. In Matthew, Jesus has no crown described, whereas in Revelation, He is crowned with many crowns

---

[84] See Quick Bite 29 – The Armies in Heaven

6. In Matthew, the emphasis is upon gathering the elect, whereas in Revelation it's about judging and making war

7. In Matthew, there is the element of surprise, for He will come like a thief in the night[85], but in Revelation, there is no element of surprise, in fact the Kings of the earth go to make war with the Lamb[86]

As we can see, there are numerous differences between these two passages. The key to understanding what is taking place is by looking at the name of the Lord for He has many names, but a biblical principle is that each name of God, reveals an aspect of who He is. For example: when the Israelites came out of Egypt after three days in the wilderness, they were desperate for water, but the waters at Marah (ma-rar) were bitter, so the Lord healed the waters to reveal to them that His name was Jehovah Rapha meaning *"I AM the Lord who heals you"*[87].

> *The names used of Jesus in the two passages of Matthew 24 and Revelation 19 reveal to us in what capacity He is coming.*

The title *'King of Kings and Lord and Lords'* in Revelation 19 is used because He is returning to reign. Whereas the title *'Son of Man'* used in Matthew is primarily because Jesus is returning as the Saviour.

---

[85] But know this, that if the master of the house had known in what watch the thief would come, he would have watched, and would not have suffered his house to be broken up. (Matthew 24:43).

[86] These shall make war with the Lamb, and the Lamb shall overcome them: for he is Lord of lords, and King of kings: and they that are with him are called, and chosen, and faithful. (Revelation 17:14).

[87] Exodus 15:22-27.

QB32 Unravelling the Rapture (Part 3)

In our studies so far looking at the end times, I have wanted to establish some foundational markers that will serve to provide us with a framework upon which we can begin to add the various pieces of the eschatological puzzle. We've been taking our time because it's important to lay a solid foundation and bed these underlying principles down. Otherwise once we begin to add the weight of other events, if the foundation is not strong, it will begin to crumble and we'll end up back at the beginning in our quest for understanding, and possibly even resign ourselves to thinking that the matter of the end times is simply too deep, too complicated, too controversial to warrant further time trying to understand, and instead opt for a more inconclusive, open-ended approach, that simply trusts things will work out in whatever way the Lord has determined.

But what if there were a kingdom assignment, some prophetic mandate that has been entrusted to us specifically for the days ahead? What if there is a position to occupy which gives us a unique vantage point from where we can intercede with great assertion? Then it necessitates an alignment in our understanding and spiritual perception so we can see more clearly and participate in the end-time campaign.

> *If being prepared for what lies ahead is more than a passive wait-and-see, but a pro-active equipping and*

> *training, then we must ensure we are marching to the right rhythm, we must understand where the battle lines are drawn, and what will be the key events of how the battle will unfold.*

This is my objective here: to help prepare the Bride, to give the right battle plans so she understands who she is, what she has been entrusted with and what her destiny shall be.

So far in building a foundational framework we have established that the triumphant return of the Warrior King in Revelation 19 takes place after the rapture since the Bride follows the Bridegroom out of heaven which means she is in Heaven leading up to this point. Then we examined the differences between the coming of Jesus in Revelation 19 and His appearance in Matthew 24. Just to be clear: this appearance in Matthew 24 is also a coming of Christ, let's read Matthew 24:30:

Then the sign of the Son of Man will appear in heaven, and then all the tribes of the earth will mourn, and they will see the Son of Man coming on the clouds of heaven with power and great glory.

What I am saying is that there are two separate and visible comings of the Lord: the first in which He comes as the '*Son of Man*' in Matthew 24, and the second in Revelation 19 in which He comes as the '*King of Kings and Lord of Lords*'. We know the rapture doesn't happen in Revelation 19 because Jesus is returning with His Bride, not for His Bride, but I won't make the leap just yet to say the rapture must therefore happen in Matthew 24, I don't want to make that theological jump or assumption. At this point in our journey, it is enough to establish how there are two different occasions in which

Jesus is seen as returning to the earth, although the purpose for each is very different.

The key passage on the rapture is found in 1 Thessalonians 4:13-18:

13 But I do not want you to be ignorant, brethren, concerning those who have fallen asleep, lest you sorrow as others who have no hope. 14 For if we believe that Jesus died and rose again, even so God will bring with Him those who sleep in Jesus. 15 For this we say to you by the word of the Lord, that we who are alive and remain until the coming of the Lord will by no means precede those who are asleep. 16 For the Lord Himself will descend from heaven with a shout, with the voice of an archangel, and with the trumpet of God. And the dead in Christ will rise first. 17 Then we who are alive and remain shall be caught up together with them in the clouds to meet the Lord in the air. And thus we shall always be with the Lord. 18 Therefore comfort one another with these words.

We will cover this passage in more depth, but for now the next foundational marker to be put into place and provide our framework is that the rapture happens after the resurrection. Listen to what Paul writes: *'The dead in Christ will rise first, then we who are alive and remain shall be caught up together with them'*. That's pretty clear, the dead in Christ rise first[88]. This is the resurrection and Paul said this happens first.

---

[88] If we believe the rapture is some time before the great tribulation, then we must also suppose of an earlier resurrection. This presents further challenges since scripture clearly states the resurrection will be on the 'Last Day'. "

QB33 Unravelling the Rapture (Part 4)

S ince the passage in 1 Thessalonians 4:13-18 is the core passage that teaches on the rapture and is used by both the pre-tribulation and non-pre-tribulation view, it would be worthwhile taking a little time to digest what Paul is teaching and why. 1 Thessalonians 4:13 gives us the answer to the '*why*' question, for he writes: '*But I do not want you to be ignorant, brethren, concerning those who have fallen asleep, lest you sorrow as others who have no hope*'. Here we see the reason why Paul writes the rapture passage because he doesn't want the Thessalonians to be ignorant about those who have fallen asleep, otherwise, Paul writes, they will be '*sorrowful like those who have no hope*'. Paul intends to tackle their ignorance by teaching them what they are unsure of, so they won't sorrow, on the contrary, he wants to reassure them, verse 18 reads '*Therefore comfort one another with these words*'. What words does Paul intend for them to comfort each other with? We can discern why the Thessalonians were troubled when we read what Paul wrote in 1 Thessalonians 4:14:

For if we believe that Jesus died and rose again, even so God will bring with Him those who sleep in Jesus.

And this is the will of Him who sent Me, that everyone who sees the Son and believes in Him may have everlasting life; and I will raise him up at the last day. (John 6:40 NKJV).
Jesus said to her, "Your brother will rise again." Martha said to Him, "I know that he will rise again in the resurrection at the last day." (John 11:23, 24 NKJV).

The Thessalonians were concerned about those who had died: would they be resurrected, would they be there at the glorious coming of the Lord, would they see them again? It was about their longing to be together. That's why Paul writes the way he does, he says we shall be gathered together with them. This is the assurance Paul comforts the Thessalonians with and us, for this is our hope also, that we shall see our loved ones again, those who have gone before us and are now asleep in the Lord shall arise and we shall be gathered together with them to meet the Lord in the air. What a wonderful day that will be, what a glorious triumph! For if we believe Jesus died and rose again, shall we not also believe how those who are in Him, yet asleep, shall rise also? But more than this: those you long to be reunited with shall return with the Lord when He comes. At this point of course it would be their departed souls coming with the Lord to receive their new glorified body at the impending resurrection.

Paul continues in verse 15:

For this we say to you by the word of the Lord, that we who are alive and remain until the coming of the Lord will by no means precede those who are asleep.

Paul's use of the phrase '*by the word of the Lord*', is incredibly emphatic. He's saying, these aren't my words, I didn't make this up, this is what the Lord has said, and this is His word to you, not mine: that we who are alive until the Lord's coming will by no means precede those who are asleep. '*By no means*' also places special emphasis on this point, in other words: absolutely, in no way will the dead in Christ not be raised first, the rapture comes after the resurrection not before. Did you notice something else here in verse 15? Paul writes the word of the Lord as follows: '*we who are alive and remain until the coming of the*

Lord' Paul understood those who are alive shall remain until the coming of the Lord, they wouldn't be raptured before this time, but would remain until He comes. This then is our next foundational marker: the resurrection/rapture[89] doesn't happen until the coming of the Lord[90]. Let's continue to read the rest of the passage:

16 For the Lord Himself will descend from heaven with a shout, with the voice of an archangel, and with the trumpet of God. And the dead in Christ will rise first. 17 Then we who are alive and remain shall be caught up together with them in the clouds to meet the Lord in the air.

Since we now know the resurrection/rapture happens when the Lord returns, if we can find a chronological marker for when that Day might be, then we can complete mapping out the stages of the rapture and anchor it to a specific event which can be measured. Without this kind of mapping, we are left with a *'Christ could return any time'* imminency perspective, or a secret rapture theory. So, is there a way to peg this *'coming of the Lord'* that Paul writes of in 1 Thessalonians 4 to another event that positions it securely on our

---

[89] Sine there is one reunion in the air of those who are asleep and those who are alive on the Lord's coming, we can see the resurrection/rapture as being one simultaneous event.

[90] When we talk of 'Coming', we should be quite clear. 1 Thessalonians 4:16 uses the word 'katabainō' (Strongs G2597) translated as 'descend', that is, 'The Lord Himself will descend' and it means 'to come down as celestial beings coming down to earth', or 'cast down'. It is the same word Jesus used to describe Himself as having come down from heaven (John 3:13), and as the Bread of God who has come down from heaven (John 6:33). The suggestion here is that at the time of the resurrection/rapture Jesus will come down from heaven, as in come down from heaven to earth, and not some secret or partial coming.

timeline? Sadly, we are out of time for today, so this is where we'll pick up from next time.

QB34 Unravelling the Rapture (Part 5)

Paul writes clearly in 1 Thessalonians 4:13-18 that the rapture does not occur before the resurrection, and that the resurrection happens when Christ returns. Here are verses 16,17 again:

16 For the Lord Himself will descend from heaven with a shout, with the voice of an archangel, and with the trumpet of God. And the dead in Christ will rise first. 17 Then we who are alive and remain shall be caught up together with them in the clouds to meet the Lord in the air.

This has given us some vital chronological markers in putting together a framework which we shall build upon later. The point I made last time, is that the resurrection and rapture are tied into the coming of the Lord and we asked if there was a way to peg this *'coming of the Lord'* Paul writes of in 1 Thessalonians 4 to another event which would position it securely on our timeline? Now the reason this is important is because of disputes over another suggested secret coming and rapture before the day of the Lord's arrival on full display. That's why I'm asking the question: can we peg the Lord's coming that Paul teaches, with any other event which is not disputed? If yes, then we can be confident knowing when the resurrection and rapture take place on our timeline. To find another event that relates to Paul's coming of the Lord, let's look at what he writes later in his second letter to the Thessalonians:

1 Now, brethren, concerning the coming of our Lord Jesus Christ and our gathering together to Him, we ask you, 2 not to be soon shaken in mind or troubled, either by spirit or by word or by letter, as if from us, as though the day of Christ had come. 3 Let no one deceive you by any means; for that Day will not come unless the falling away comes first, and the man of sin is revealed, the son of perdition, 4 who opposes and exalts himself above all that is called God or that is worshipped, so that he sits as God in the temple of God, showing himself that he is God. 5 Do you not remember that when I was still with you I told you these things? (2 Thessalonians 2:1-5).

On a simple, first glance, reading of this text, Paul puts the matter of the day of the Lord (or Christ as it is here) in no uncertain terms. He makes an unequivocal, indisputable statement saying that the day of Christ will not come until two things happen: First, there will be a *'falling away'*, other translations give *'the great rebellion'* or *'the apostasy'*, then secondly, *'the man of sin is revealed, the son of perdition'* (or man of lawlessness) who exalts himself above God, will sit as God in the temple. Jesus and Daniel both referred to this heinous act as the *'abomination of desolation'*.

To summarise then, Paul is saying that the day of the Lord, will not happen until after the abomination of desolation in the temple when the son of perdition is revealed. There is little doubt when this happens that we are in the Great Tribulation. Therefore, the resurrection and subsequent rapture will not happen until after this point. This would appear to shatter the pre-trib viewpoint once and for all. Paul says in no uncertain terms, *'concerning the coming of our Lord Jesus Christ and our gathering together to Him'* this will not happen until after the apostasy and the revealing of the son of perdition.

However, the pre-trib view does not dispute the day of the Lord described here will not be as Paul taught, but the point of contention is that when Paul writes in v1 '*Now, brethren, concerning the coming of our Lord Jesus Christ and our gathering together to Him*', he lists the '*coming of our Lord Jesus Christ*' as separate to '*our gathering together to Him*', implying they are two separate events, and the gathering together happens at another coming before this one. However, I believe this point is not sustainable and here's why: In the same chapter verse 5, when Paul writes, '*when I was with you I told you these things*', he refers to things he had already taught them. Now we know from his first letter what he taught. We learnt in Quick Bite 33 Paul explicitly teaches the '*coming of the Lord*' and '*our gathering together*' are not two separate events, but happen simultaneously, they are not separated by time. Therefore, when Paul teaches in 2 Thessalonians 2 the timing of the day of Christ is after the apostasy and the abomination of desolation, he is including the resurrection and rapture.[91]

---

[91] The rapture position and timing I have described should be the end of the matter, as there is no disputing the clarity of Paul's exposition. Indeed, he deliberately makes it clear because this is his apologetic on the rapture and second coming, in response to the concerns and questions posed by the Thessalonian believers. To keep the pre-trib view alive, one has to suggest that there is yet another coming of the Lord that precedes His return as either King of Kings in Revelation 19, or as the Son of Man in Matthew 24. This of course would be forced to say the least: first, because there is no other explicit text that describes another coming other than those above, and second, because it still doesn't address Paul's exposition that the resurrection immediately precedes the rapture, so they are simultaneous. In order to keep the pre-trib argument alive, there are those then who would suggest there must be other earlier resurrections, and we deviate further away from what is actually stated, to theories and suppositions. Hopefully you can see how dangerous this is, rather than just let the scripture speak for itself.

QB35 Unravelling the Rapture (Part 6)

It's time to connect the dots! We have seen that when Paul speaks of the rapture, aka *'the gathering'*, he has in mind the *'Day of the Lord'* also known as the *'Day of Christ'* and in case there is any doubt, he clarifies that this day happens after the *'abomination of desolation'* when the *'son of perdition'*, the *'man of lawlessness'* is revealed. I have shared previously about two separate occasions when Jesus will come again, first in Matthew 24 as the *'Son of Man'*, and second in Revelation 19 as the *'King of Kings and Lord of Lords'*. We have seen how these two events differ in their description, and I have proposed they are not the same[92]. By the time we get to Revelation 19, the Bride has already been raptured, because we see her in heaven, receiving fine linen to wear, and following the Lord out of heaven when He returns to judge and make war. This leaves us with Matthew 24 as being the only remaining candidate combining *'a coming'* with a *'rapture/gathering'*, which happens sometime after the abomination of desolation. Let's look a bit closer at Matthew 24 and see how it compares to Pauls teaching in Thessalonians:

15 So when you see the abomination of desolation spoken of by the prophet Daniel, standing in the holy place (let the reader understand),16 then let those who are in Judea flee to the mountains. 17 Let the one who is on the housetop not go down to take what is in his house, 18 and let the one who is

---

[92] See Quick Bite 31.

in the field not turn back to take his cloak. 19 And alas for women who are pregnant and for those who are nursing infants in those days! 20 Pray that your flight may not be in winter or on a Sabbath. 21 For then there will be great tribulation, such as has not been from the beginning of the world until now, no, and never will be. 22 And if those days had not been cut short, no human being would be saved. But for the sake of the elect those days will be cut short. 23 Then if anyone says to you, 'Look, here is the Christ!' or 'There he is!' do not believe it. 24 For false christs and false prophets will arise and perform great signs and wonders, so as to lead astray, if possible, even the elect. 25 See, I have told you beforehand. 26 So, if they say to you, 'Look, he is in the wilderness,' do not go out. If they say, 'Look, he is in the inner rooms,' do not believe it. 27 For as the lightning comes from the east and shines as far as the west, so will be the coming of the Son of Man. 28 Wherever the corpse is, there the vultures will gather. 29 "Immediately after the tribulation of those days the sun will be darkened, and the moon will not give its light, and the stars will fall from heaven, and the powers of the heavens will be shaken. 30 Then will appear in heaven the sign of the Son of Man, and then all the tribes of the earth will mourn, and they will see the Son of Man coming on the clouds of heaven with power and great glory. 31 And he will send out his angels with a loud trumpet call, and they will gather his elect from the four winds, from one end of heaven to the other.

There are a great many similarities between Paul's teaching in 1 and 2 Thessalonians and Jesus' teaching in Matthew 24 and 25. To point out a few:

1. Both Jesus and Paul define the gathering after the abomination of desolation, and after the tribulation.

2. Both Jesus and Paul teach Jesus will come again on the clouds.

3. They both refer to the apostasy and falling away, and

4. They both mention the playing of a trumpet.

Yet even with such conspicuous parallels between the two, it is still not enough for the astute student to say just because similarities exist doesn't mean they are necessarily describing the same thing, and I would have to agree! Indeed, the pre-tribulation view is that the gathering in Matthew 24 is not the rapture spoken of by Paul in Thessalonians, and this debate has persisted for a long time. So what can be done to reconcile the differences which can so easily divide the Body of Christ today? I am not looking to exert one viewpoint above another by shouting louder metaphorically, no! We must approach this with utmost love and respect for all. Let us be those who listen to each other, especially when what they have to say can be supported with good biblical exegesis. It's not about defending a particular position and scoring points, that's not where I'm coming from, my objective here isn't to take sides, or to persuade anyone to change theirs, no let that be left to the Holy Spirit to grant us all wisdom and understanding as we fervently study the scriptures with an open heart and mind.

My objective is to give a biblical rationale of the Call2Come viewpoint so that people know what we believe and why. I don't like the labels pre-trib, mid-trib, post-trib or pre-wrath, though they may help to consolidate groups of people with similar views, they can also serve to alienate us from each other.

> *I believe we need a new paradigm, a new approach, lest we continue going around in circles with no resolution. Is there such a way forward, a unified position that will draw us all together? I believe there is!*

It will take us all, laying down our positions and opinions, to embrace a new design. You will have heard me say by now, that I believe the key to unlocking the end times is the Bride, and next time I will share how the Bridal paradigm can open up a whole new perspective on the gathering in Matthew 24.

QB36 Who Are the Elect? (Part 1)

29 Immediately after the tribulation of those days the sun will be darkened, and the moon will not give its light, and the stars will fall from heaven, and the powers of the heavens will be shaken. 30 Then will appear in heaven the sign of the Son of Man, and then all the tribes of the earth will mourn, and they will see the Son of Man coming on the clouds of heaven with power and great glory. 31 And he will send out his angels with a loud trumpet call, and they will gather his elect from the four winds, from one end of heaven to the other. (Matthew 24:29-31).

Today I want us to pause and reflect for a moment on what it really means to adopt a bridal perspective on matters of the end times. We know from church history, there has been much controversy and disagreement over matters of the future, at times aggressive argument, even leading to denominational splits within the Body of Christ. Was this ever the Lord's intention to leave us in a quandary over such things, was He not always clear in His teaching? Even when using parables so

they may be ever hearing but never understanding (Luke 8:10).

He would then explain the meaning to His disciples, and the Gospel writers would give us the interpretation. The problem over Matthew

24 would never arise if the Lord didn't use the term *'the elect'* as He does in verse 31:

And he will send out his angels with a loud trumpet call, and they will gather his elect from the four winds, from one end of heaven to the other. (Matthew 24:31).

If only the Lord had said *'the angels will gather the tribes of Israel'*, then there would be little doubt what He meant. Similarly, if He had said *'the angels will gather the church'*, then we would also be clear. The debate hangs on the identification of who Jesus meant when He said *'His Elect'*[93]. We have no record of the disciples asking Jesus about this; I strongly suspect they knew exactly who the *'Elect'* were. The Greek word for *'Elect'* is *'eklektos'* (*ek-lek-tos*) and means *'chosen by God'*. Certainly, there is no shortage of Old Testament passages which refer to Israel as the Chosen (or Elect) of God. For example:

For you are a people holy to the LORD your God. He has chosen you to be his people, prized above all others on the face of the earth. (Deuteronomy 7:6 NET).

For the LORD has chosen Jacob for himself, Israel as his own possession. (Psalms 135:4 ESV).

These and many other verses tell us Israel are the elect (or chosen) of God. Furthermore, Paul writes in Romans 11:1,2a[ESV]:

I ask, then, has God rejected his people? By no means! For I myself am an Israelite, a descendant of Abraham, a member

---

[93] Note Jesus calls them His Elect. This is a subtle but important point. When considering the Elect, we should understand that they are His Elect, that is those chosen by Jesus as His own.

of the tribe of Benjamin. 2 God has not rejected his people whom he foreknew.

What are we to make of this? The answer comes when we understand the Elect to be His Bride! Had Jesus said, *'the angels will gather Israel'* or *'the angels will gather the church'* we would have taken it to be mutually exclusive as we do today and argue depending upon whether we are *'pre-trib'* or *'post-trib'*, for the Elect to be either Israel or the church but not both. As though there were two plans of salvation: one for Israel and one for the church. Two covenants; one for Israel and one for the church. Or even two elects or two chosen peoples with two different gatherings[94]. But this is not true. There has only been and will ever be one chosen people, one elect and one covenant. There has only been and will ever be one plan of salvation for both Jew and Gentile[95].

> *The Bridal mind cannot separate Jew from Gentile, she has been healed in Christ to think from a One New Man perspective.*

When we take a side, we are not seeing as the Bride should. She is indelibly changed to think differently, to think as her Bridegroom thinks and see how He sees, and what He sees is His Bride! All the promises the church has received have come to her through the covenant God made with Israel because the New Covenant is made with Israel[96]. Whatever blessing we have is only because we have

---

[94] As in dispensationalism which separates Israel from the Church, or worse replacement theology which believes the church has replaced Israel, and therefore all the promises, covenants are transferred to the church
[95] For I am not ashamed of the gospel of Christ, for it is the power of God to salvation for everyone who believes, for the Jew first and also for the Greek. (Romans 1:16).
[96] see Quick Bite 19.

been grafted into the Olive Tree. The promise of salvation and for a Messiah was made to Israel. The promise to be gathered was made to Israel. What promise did God ever make separately to the church for her to raptured in a way that would tear her apart from the tree? He has one plan of salvation, one resurrection of the righteous, and one gathering of the Elect, His Bride! Now that we are grafted in, are we to be torn away and leave the Bride upon the Earth? By no means! We are not the Bride on our own, but corporately together.

> *When Jesus comes for His Bride, He will not take her one member at a time, but as a whole.*

Now I've just made some pretty radical points, so let me back this up with scripture which we'll find in Matthew 22. I'm sure you'll remember the parable of the wedding banquet when the imposter was thrown outside because he didn't have the wedding garments on, well Jesus concluded His teaching in verse 14 saying:

For many are called, but few are chosen. (Matthew 22:14).

And what was the word for chosen? It is the exact same word as the *'elect'* the *'eklektos'*.[97]

---

[97] Jesus' use of the word 'elect' was not exclusive to Matthew 24. We can understand who Jesus meant when He referred to the 'elect' by studying how He used the word elsewhere, as in the parable of the wedding banquet when the 'elect' are those who will be at the wedding.

QB37 Who Are the Elect? (Part 2)

29 Immediately after the tribulation of those days the sun will be darkened, and the moon will not give its light; the stars will fall from heaven, and the powers of the heavens will be shaken. 30 Then the sign of the Son of Man will appear in heaven, and then all the tribes of the earth will mourn, and they will see the Son of Man coming on the clouds of heaven with power and great glory. 31 And He will send His angels with a great sound of a trumpet, and they will gather together His elect from the four winds, from one end of heaven to the other.
(Matthew 24:29-31).

Agreement over the identity of those being gathered by the Lord's angels in this well-known passage has been the subject of much debate and controversy for a long time. I believe the key to understanding this passage and to approaching eschatology in general, is to do so from the Bridal paradigm, which is inclusive of Israel. The core issue is over the term '*the Elect*', although it's worth pointing out the passage doesn't say '*the Elect*' but '*His Elect*'. The word '*Elect*' is the word '*eklektos*' and simply means '*chosen*'. In other words, this passage in Matthew 24 when speaking of those being gathered means the ones Jesus has chosen. It's really not my intention to argue for a particular viewpoint, as I believe there are problems with any viewpoint, whether it be pre-trib, mid-trib, pre-wrath or post-trib. Unless any view is approached from a renewed bridal mindset it will invariably fail to see the bigger picture of the Bride with the Bridegroom who returns to reign upon planet earth. The Bride isn't a doctrine to tag onto the end of the eschatological timeline from Revelation 19 onwards, but she is our corporate identity, and her footprints are to be seen throughout all scripture, especially as we move into the end times; because it's as we approach the end that the Bride becomes increasingly evident, as her final preparations are being made.

> *My passion is for the Bride to be ready, to make clear her critical role to play in the end times which necessitates her presence upon the earth during the tribulation.*

But before I can move on to share more about those things, it's important to establish this crucial identification of the '*Elect*' or should I say, '*His Elect*'? To do this is not difficult if we approach scripture as we should with an open mind, not looking to put anything into the text that it doesn't say, but just letting the text speak for itself. We must let scripture interpret scripture rather than filter the interpretation through our prejudices and suppositions because we're not looking for scripture to support what we already believe but calibrate what we believe against what the scripture explicitly teaches. A classic example of this is the pre-trib supposition that the Elect must be Israel because the church would have been raptured before the tribulation. But the text doesn't say Israel, it says '*His Elect*'. In this case, the pre-trib view forces a conclusion on the verse to support its position and doesn't allow the verse to speak for itself. I hope you can see how dangerous that can be. The right approach is to step back, separate what is being said from what is not, and let scripture interpret scripture. So here's what I believe is a good exegesis of the term '*His Elect*'. First of all:

1. Does Jesus use the word *'eklektos'* (chosen, elect) to refer to Israel elsewhere? The answer is no. When Jesus meant to refer to Israel He did so directly. For example:

These twelve Jesus sent out, instructing them, "Go nowhere among the Gentiles and enter no town of the Samaritans, but go rather to the lost sheep of the house of Israel. (Matthew 10:5,6 ESV).

There isn't any scripture in which Jesus refers to Israel as *'His Elect'*.

2. Does Jesus use the word *'eklektos'* (chosen, elect) elsewhere in His teaching? Yes. When He teaches the parable of the wedding banquet, (remember the one who was found at the banquet without the wedding garments on was thrown into outer darkness), Jesus said

many are called but few are chosen (Elect). (Matthew 22:14).

The Elect are those who shall attend the Marriage Banquet, and as I have shared in our earlier study of the ten virgins, these are the Bride, for the terms *'guest'*, *'virgin'*, *'friend of the bridegroom'* are all interchangeable depending upon the underlying principle being taught at the time.

3. Do we know who Jesus' disciples saw as being *'His Elect'*? The answer is yes we do. Amongst those closest to the Lord was the Apostle Peter. Listen to what he writes in his first letter:

1 Peter, an apostle of Jesus Christ, To the pilgrims of the Dispersion in Pontus, Galatia, Cappadocia, Asia, and Bithynia, 2 elect (eklektos) according to the foreknowledge of God the Father, in sanctification of the

> Spirit, for obedience and sprinkling of the blood of Jesus
> Christ: Grace to you and peace be multiplied.
> (1 Peter 1:1-2).

Surely, Peter's view on the Elect should be able to persuade us once and for all; since his view is a reflection of what Jesus taught Him. It's very significant how Peter begins his letter, for he writes to *'the pilgrims of the Dispersion'*, which was a term originally used of the Jews who had been scattered into different lands because of the Roman invasion. Does this mean Peter saw the Elect as the scattered tribes of Israel? Well, I'll address that question and more next time.

QB38 Who Are the Elect? (Part 3)

Peter, an apostle of Jesus Christ, To the pilgrims of the Dispersion in Pontus, Galatia, Cappadocia, Asia, and Bithynia, elect (eklektos) according to the foreknowledge of God the Father, in sanctification of the Spirit, for obedience and sprinkling of the blood of Jesus Christ: Grace to you and peace be multiplied.
(1 Peter 1:1-2).

When Peter writes his first letter, he addresses it to the *'pilgrims of the Dispersion'*. This familiar term was ascribed to the scattered Jews who had been displaced out of Israel into other lands because of the Roman invasion. Then in verse 2, Peter describes them as *'elect according to the foreknowledge of God'*. It would appear at first glance that Peter is writing specifically to the Jews, but if we continue reading the letter, it becomes clear who he is addressing. This identification of Peter's readers is important because it links into our wider discussion of who are the Elect.

> As one of Jesus' closest disciples, Peter's testimony of the Elect would be in harmony with the Lord's, so his understanding of the Elect helps us to identify those to be gathered immediately after the great tribulation which Jesus spoke of in Matthew 24:31.

Peter writes:

knowing that you were ransomed from the futile ways inherited from your forefathers, not with perishable things such as silver or gold (1 Peter 1:18 ESV).

and later,

who once were not a people but are now the people of God, who had not obtained mercy but now have obtained mercy. (1 Peter 2:10).

Peter gives us a window through which we can look closer at his readers. He describes them as *'ransomed from the futile ways of their forefathers'*. Does this sound like the Jews or the Gentiles? Or what about those *'who once were not a people but are now the people of God'*, to whom does Peter refer? The apostle Paul writes similarly:

11 Therefore remember that you, once Gentiles in the flesh-- who are called Uncircumcision by what is called the Circumcision made in the flesh by hands-- 12 that at that time you were without Christ, being aliens from the commonwealth of Israel and strangers from the covenants of promise, having no hope and without God in the world. 13 But now in Christ Jesus you who once were far off have been brought near by the blood of Christ. (Ephesians 2:11-13).

When Peter writes, he does so to those who were not a people, but had been ransomed, to be the people of God, So yes. I do believe Peter includes Gentile believers when he writes, but more than that, His perspective has changed, for he no longer differentiates between Jew and Gentile but sees them as the Lord does, the Elect. Wonderfully inspired by the Holy Spirit, he calls them *'pilgrims of the dispersion'*, and *'elect of God'*, and in so doing, Peter is grafting in the wild olive branch into the native olive tree that is Israel. Wow, that's important, because like Paul, Peter is saying there is a *'commonwealth of Israel'*, he is identifying Gentile believers with their Hebrew roots! The underlying message of Peter is to encourage the '*Elect*' around the known world to persevere through great hardship, persecution and suffering. For in their endurance they follow the footsteps of Jesus who suffered and died for them so they might be saved.

Peter proposes solidarity in suffering shared jointly by Jew and Gentile because there is only one Elect. Whatever path the gentile church takes that separates them from Israel is not one ordained by God. There isn't a separate plan of God for a Gentile church, no, if she is to benefit from any benevolence of Divine mercy, it is only because she has been grafted into Israel. All the covenants and promises are made to Israel, not to the gentile church. Here's what Paul writes Romans 9:4[ESV]:

They are Israelites, and to them belong the adoption, the glory, the covenants, the giving of the law, the worship, and the promises.

So, to answer our question: Who are the Elect? I think Peter gives a great answer when he writes in 1 Peter 2:9[NKJV]:

But you are a chosen (eklektos, Elect) generation, a royal priesthood, a holy nation, His own special people, that you may proclaim the praises of Him who called you out of darkness into His marvellous light.

I'll finish by drawing together the points I made last time and just now. Jesus never referred to Israel as the Elect, He always spoke of Israel directly, but He did use the term Elect when speaking of the chosen to be at the Wedding Banquet[98] *(please refer to the footnote here, because it shows how Jesus redefined who He saw as His elect).* Peter understood the Elect of God to be inclusive of both Jew and Gentile, and he created solidarity in suffering between the two. Ultimately

---

[98] The parable of the Wedding Banquet we find in Matthew 22 holds key principles to be understood if we are to gain a proper understanding of the Bride and indeed who the Elect are. Firstly, note the context in which Jesus taught this parable: It was in admonishing the chief priests and elders (Matthew 21:23) who had continued to vehemently oppose Jesus. He used the parable to teach how Israel had not accepted the wedding invitation sent out to them and therefore the wedding invitation had been sent out to others (that is, the Gentiles). Through this parable we can see how there is only one wedding, and that the wedding planned for Israel had been opened up to receive others into the gathering, namely the Gentiles. This supports the principle I've been sharing in these Quick Bites that there is only one Bride and one wedding. It removes the notion of a separate wedding for Israel and one for the church, or the Father has a bride and the Son has another bride. Such suppositions are short-lived when weighed against scripture. Secondly, when considering the 'Elect' it is not those who had been originally invited (that is Israel) who qualify for this description, but rather those who are rightly dressed in their wedding garments. To me, this parable clearly reveals who Jesus meant when speaking of the 'Elect'. He was directly confronting the attitude held by the religious leaders who considered themselves the 'elect' and the 'chosen' of God, and instead Jesus was redefining who the 'Elect' were, not through their ancestry, but by their faith in Him. This confronting of the religious attitude over their rights or inherited identity is more than once strongly countered by Jesus. Here Jesus negates their identity as the 'Elect', elsewhere he rebuts their confidence to be children of Abraham.

But when he saw many of the Pharisees and Sadducees coming to his baptism, he said to them, "Brood of vipers! Who warned you to flee from the wrath to come? Therefore, bear fruits worthy of repentance, and do not think to say to yourselves, 'We have Abraham as our father.' For I say to you that God is able to raise up children to Abraham from these stones. And even now the axe is laid to the root of the trees. Therefore, every tree which does not bear good fruit is cut down and thrown into the fire." (Matthew 3:7-10) see also John 8:37-42.

Peter describes the Elect as a chosen '*eklektos*' generation, a royal priesthood and a holy nation, God's own special people. I believe this to be good biblical exegesis letting scripture speak for itself, and using scripture to interpret scripture, and not eisegesis putting something into the text that isn't there. I hope you'll agree with me. We've taken time to unpack this because it's an important marker on our timeline. At this stage, since we have identified the Elect, or I should say '*His Elect*', I am happy to connect Matthew 24:29-31 and 1 Thessalonians 4:13-18 since they both refer to the same group of people, '*we who are alive and remain until the coming of the Lord.*'

QB39 If the Days of the Tribulation Will Be Shortened, How Long Will They Be?

In recent studies, we have unpacked the meaning of the Elect, so we may identify those Jesus speaks of in Matthew 24:31:

31 And He will send His angels with a great sound of a trumpet, and they will gather together His elect from the four winds, from one end of heaven to the other.

From our studies, we now know who '*His Elect*' are, and as we discovered there was no great mystery, no complex solution, the answer is as the text says; His chosen! That's you and I, His Bride, the One New Man, which Peter beautifully describes as:

a chosen (eklektos, Elect) generation, a royal priesthood, a holy nation, His own special people, that you may proclaim the praises of Him who called you out of darkness into His marvellous light (1 Peter 2:9 NKJV).

We also know from Matthew 24:29 [99] that we shall be gathered immediately after the tribulation when the sun will be darkened and the moon will not shine. This is a direct reference to Joel's prophecy who writes:

---

[99] Immediately after the tribulation of those days the sun will be darkened, and the moon will not give its light; the stars will fall from heaven, and the powers of the heavens will be shaken. (Matthew 24:29).

The sun shall be turned to darkness, and the moon to blood, before the great and awesome day of the LORD comes. (Joel 2:31 ESV).

But is that the end of the matter? Maybe not, for we may probe deeper and say '*well, when will the great tribulation end? How long will it be?*' This question seems valid because Jesus himself taught:

And unless those days were shortened, no flesh would be saved; but for the elect's sake those days will be shortened. (Matthew 24:22 NKJV).

Does this mean the gathering of the Elect takes place sooner than expected? If the days are shortened, how long will the great tribulation be? The prophet Daniel was given the answer to this question in Daniel 7:25 and Daniel 12:7 concerning the apocalyptic visions he saw:

He (that is the anti-Christ) shall speak words against the Most High, he shall wear out (harass) the saints (holy ones) of the Most High, And shall think to change the times and the law; and they (the saints[100] or holy ones) shall be given into his hand for a time and times and half a time. (Daniel 7:25 ESV).

Who are the saints (or holy ones) of the Most High referred to here? Many will say these are Israel, but what does the text say, let's allow the scripture to speak to us and read further in verse 27:

Then the kingdom and dominion, And the greatness of the kingdoms under the whole heaven, Shall be given to the people, the saints of the Most High. His kingdom is an

---

[100] The Septuagint doesn't say saints but power.

everlasting kingdom, And all dominions shall serve and obey Him.

In this verse we are told who the saints are — they are the ones to whom the dominion, and greatness of the kingdoms under all of heaven will be given. And who is it who will share the Kingdom with the Lord? Paul answers this question when he writes to Timothy:

If we endure, we shall also reign with Him. If we deny Him, He also will deny us. (2 Timothy 2:12).

It is the Elect, who are destined to reign with the Lord. Do you see how difficult it is when we try to separate Israel from the church? It doesn't work. If the church is to reign with the Lord, then she must place herself into the context of Daniel 7:25, or if the church says no no this passage relates to the nation of Israel, then she can't claim the blessing promised here to reign. But why does it have to be one or the other? That's what we've inherited through different theological systems which separate Israel and the Gentile church like dispensationalism. That's why the Bridal mindset is critical here, because it sees the Bride, the One New Man, and doesn't make the distinction. This is a profound mystery and a miracle of Divine Grace. We hear much talk of 'reformation', but reformation merely re-forms, what we need is beyond reformation. We need transformation. Not a re-form but a change of form, a transform.

> *The church can't take the promises made to Israel, and not be identified with her also. She can't take the promise of being gathered which was made to Israel and change the timing of when that promise would be fulfilled.*

It's all or nothing, we're either in or out, not a pick and mix theology, taking the assurances and promises made to Israel, without the solidarity of standing with her through the tough times ahead. So when are the Elect gathered? They are gathered after the great tribulation, which as Daniel tells us is *'for a time and times and half a time'*[101] that is 1260 days after the revealing of the Anti-Christ.

Finally then, when Jesus said:

but for the elect's sake, those days will be shortened. (meaning cut off as in amputate) (Matthew 24:22).

He did not mean Daniel was wrong, or there had been a revision to the dates or duration of tribulation, but instead the meaning of those days being shortened, or amputated, is that the wickedness of the Beast would not be permitted to take its full course, those days will be cut off, the short reign of the Anti-Christ will be terminated before his plans succeed.

---

[101] Scholars agree that the phrase 'time and times and half a time' is three and a half years, forty-two months or 1260 days. All these phrases are used interchangeably, for example:

Then the woman fled into the wilderness, where she has a place prepared by God, that they should feed her there one thousand two hundred and sixty days. (Revelation 12:6).

But the woman was given two wings of a great eagle, that she might fly into the wilderness to her place, where she is nourished for a time and times and half a time, from the presence of the serpent. (Revelation 12:14).

And he was given a mouth speaking great things and blasphemies, and he was given authority to continue for forty-two months. (Revelation 13:5).

QB40 The Day of the Lord

There was a day that Isaiah longed to see when he writes:

Oh that you would rend the heavens and come down, that the mountains might quake at your presence—as when fire kindles brushwood and the fire causes water to boil— to make your name known to your adversaries, and that the nations might tremble at your presence! (Isaiah 64:1,2 ESV).

Well, his prayer is finally answered at the climax of this current era, when all speculation will be answered about who Jesus really is, for Jesus will return in full view, and just as Isaiah prayed, His name will be made known to His adversaries, and the nations will tremble at His presence. When will this happen? This has been the subject of great debate since Jesus ascended from the Mount of Olives in Acts 1. But even outside the church, the world seems to have a fascination with some sort of apocalypse, an end of the world scenario which is the fashion of so many books and films. Astronomers point us to the signs in the heavens, with such phenomena as planet alignment, blood moons, comets and precession of the equinoxes[102], whilst archaeologists and historians bring us artefacts like the Mayan calendar which some argue has significance and implications today. Many religious leaders have made predictions of dates that have

---

[102] https://en.wikipedia.org/wiki/Axial_precession

come and gone over the centuries [103], the fact is, despite the abundance of predictions for the end of the world, in all these things, we are still here. But there will be a day like no other when the heavens shall be rolled back, and lightning will split the sky. And unlike the arrival in obscurity of Jesus' First Coming, when He comes again as the Son of Man riding on the clouds, His glory shall be seen throughout the whole earth. What a day that will be. Jesus describes in Matthew 24:29 how *'the sun will be darkened, the moon will not give its light, the stars will fall from heaven and the powers of the heavens will be shaken'*. This parallels Joel's prophecy and is called the *'Day of the Lord'*.

The sun shall be turned to darkness, and the moon to blood, before the great and awesome day of the LORD comes. (Joel 2:31 ESV).

This passage in Joel we find being fulfilled on the opening of the sixth seal. Here's what Revelation 6:12-14 says:

When he opened the sixth seal, I looked, and behold, there was a great earthquake, and the sun became black as sackcloth, the full moon became like blood, 13 and the stars of the sky fell to the earth as the fig tree sheds its winter fruit when shaken by a gale. 14 The sky vanished like a scroll that is being rolled up, and every mountain and island was removed from its place.

So quick recap: When Jesus comes as the Son of Man on the clouds to gather *'His Elect'*, this is known as the *'Day of the Lord'* when the

---

[103] https://www.britannica.com/list/10-failed-doomsday-predictions

sun will be darkened and the moon will become like blood. But listen to what happens next continuing from verse 15:

15 Then the kings of the earth and the great ones and the generals and the rich and the powerful, and everyone, slave and free, hid themselves in the caves and among the rocks of the mountains, 16 calling to the mountains and rocks, "Fall on us and hide us from the face of him who is seated on the throne, and from the wrath of the Lamb, 17 for the great day of their wrath has come, and who can stand?" (Revelation 6:15-17).

I'd like to highlight this very important point. Did you notice it says how everyone will try to hide away from Him who is seated on the throne and from the wrath of the Lamb? Why? Because the great day of their wrath has come. Let that point sink in for a moment. The day of wrath comes on the Day of the Lord, which is the same time when the Elect are Gathered. It means those who will be raptured although they will endure the great tribulation they shall escape the wrath of God, because the wrath of God has not come until this point. Surely it can't be that simple, can it? What about all the trumpets and bowls? Something doesn't add up, have we missed something here? Do we need to go back to the eschatological drawing board and start again? How can the Elect, go through the great tribulation and still escape the wrath of God which is so clearly a part of Revelation? Well, I'll answer these questions next time.

QB41 The Wrath of God

W e've reached an important milestone in our studies which all centre around the Day of the Lord. There are numerous things which will all happen on that day, the subject of which could fill many books, so my challenge is to present as best I can the nuggets of truth found in scripture to help piece together the end-time puzzle from a Bridal perspective in this Quick Bite format.

Last time I asked the question: if the Elect are gathered immediately after the great tribulation, how is it they escape the wrath of God? As incredible as it may seem, is it possible the wrath of God begins on the Day of the Lord when the Elect are gathered and not before? That during the tribulation of the Elect, which will last 1260 days, the wrath of God has not yet been unleashed. I realise this may be a bit of a wrecking ball to many currently held opinions, but it highlights the importance to tenaciously separate our own thoughts from what scripture actually says. At any point, it's so easy to allow our preconceptions to distort our understanding of the Biblical narrative. Let's look to see what the scripture does say, and perhaps even more importantly what it doesn't say.

Here's what Zephaniah says about the day of the Lord:

14 The great day of the LORD is near; It is near and hastens quickly. The noise of the day of the LORD is bitter; There the mighty men shall cry out. 15 That day is a day of wrath, A day of trouble and distress, A day of devastation

and desolation, A day of darkness and gloominess, A day of clouds and thick darkness, (Zephaniah 1:14-15 NKJV).

From this passage and many others, the Day of the Lord is associated with wrath. We know from Revelation 6:12 this day begins on the opening of the sixth seal when everyone tries to hide:

For the great day of His wrath has come, and who is able to stand? (Revelation 6:17).

Furthermore, we've established the Day of the Lord is when the Elect are gathered, and in Quick Bite 36 to 38 I've explained how the Elect are the chosen Bride, the One New Man. The difficulty we have is trying to reconcile: *'if the Elect are not gathered until after the tribulation, how is it they escape God's wrath because surely the tribulation is a demonstration, an outpouring of God's wrath?'* Where do we place the sequences of the seven seals, the seven trumpets and the seven bowls on the eschatological timeline? If these sequences relate to God's wrath it creates a conundrum, because as Paul writes:

For God did not appointed us to wrath.
(1 Thessalonians 5:9).

There's a real dilemma here. It's one reason why the pre-trib view arose; to be able to answer the question: *'how can the Elect go through the tribulation and not be appointed unto wrath?'* Its answer was to separate the church from Israel.

To resolve this issue, we need to be precise about how the Bible connects wrath with the sequence of seals, trumpets and bowls. This is a crucial point in the discussion, because the supposition is that the seals, trumpets and bowls are about the wrath of God. So let's check that supposition to make sure it's correct before we go any further. In the New Testament, there are two Greek words used for '*wrath*'. The first is the word '*orge*' (ar-gay) and means '*anger, vengeance, indignation, and punishment*'. The second is the word '*thymos*' (thoo-maas) and means '*passion, heat, boiling up anger soon subsiding*', there are derivatives, but these are the two root words for '*wrath*'. Interestingly, by the simple use of a good concordance, you'll find the first mention of either '*orge*' or '*thymos*' wrath in the book of Revelation is not found until Revelation 6:16,17:

16 and they said to the mountains and rocks, "Fall on us and hide us from the face of Him who sits on the throne and from the wrath (orge) of the Lamb! 17 "For the great day of His wrath (orge) has come, and who is able to stand?".

Then the second occurrence of either '*orge*' or '*thymos*' wrath is found after the blowing of the seventh trumpet in Revelation 11:18:

The nations were angry, and Your wrath (orge) has come, And the time of the dead, that they should be judged, And that You should reward Your servants the prophets and the saints, And those who fear Your name, small and great, And should destroy those who destroy the earth.

Remember, we're leaving out our preconceptions of what we think the wrath of God is, and simply letting the scriptures speak to us. By doing this we observe neither '*orge*' or '*thymos*' wrath appears in Revelation until the sixth seal which we already know is the Day of the Lord after the tribulation of the Elect. Secondly, we also note the trumpet sequence isn't connected with '*wrath*' either: it's not until the seventh trumpet is sounded when wrath shall come as Revelation 11:18 tells us:

The nations were angry, and Your wrath has come.

Regarding the sixth seal I believe it's clear the wrath of God had not come until this point, otherwise why hadn't everyone tried to hide before? There is a direct cause and effect here; the wrath of the Lamb has come and therefore everyone is terrified and try to escape. Regarding the seventh trumpet, the timing of wrath could be seen as earlier, as some translations put it *'your wrath came'*, and therefore the text on its own is ambiguous. But when going to the original ancient Greek construction and verb tense of *'your wrath has come'*, found in both the seventh trumpet and the sixth seal, we find an exact match. In other words, just as with the sixth seal the wrath of God will only come at this point, so also the seventh trumpet marks the coming of God's wrath. Now in no way do I mean to lessen the dreadful and horrific things which will take place during the seals and trumpets, that's not my point. The issue is being really careful to understand the application of God's wrath in the context of the tribulation and keep clearly within the Biblical narrative. We'll carry on with this next time.

QB42 The Seals, Trumpets and Bowls (Part 1)

The question we are currently asking in our studies is not whether the wrath of God has been reserved for the Day of the Lord (for in Quick Bite 41 we have already seen how this is the case), but how the seals, trumpets and bowls fit into the picture. This is a point of great contention and difficulty. The two main positions on this are either the three sequences are progressive, that is the seals are followed by the trumpets which are followed by the bowls, one sequence following the other, or the three sequences are simultaneous, that is the first seal, first trumpet and the first bowl happen at the same time, then the second seal, trumpet and bowl take place and so on. Obviously, they both can't be correct, so which one is right, or is there another possibility? I believe there is. What I have proposed so far is that the sixth seal and seventh trumpet converge at the same point, the Day of the Lord, when the Elect are gathered, but I do not support the bowls also converge on that day.

The progressive view would say, '*Hey, wait a minute, the sequence of seven trumpets doesn't begin until Revelation 8:2 which is after the seventh seal in Revelation 8:1.*' Since the Bridal view I'm presenting here must stand up to scrutiny, I'll answer this objection now. So here is the text that supports the progressive view:

And when he opened the seventh seal, there was silence in heaven for about half an hour. 2 And I saw the seven angels who stand before God, and seven trumpets were given to them. (Revelation 8:1,2 LEB).

True, the reference to the seven trumpets is made after the reference to the seventh seal, which if we saw the Book of Revelation as entirely linear in the chronology of the events it describes, then yes, we would have to accept the sequence of trumpets does not begin until after the seventh seal. The problem with this approach is that the Book of Revelation isn't entirely linear but thematic. Furthermore, it does not always place those themes or events in chronological order but rather in the order John received them, or at least in the order he wrote them down. An example of this is Revelation 7:14 NKJV:

And I said to him, "Sir, you know." So he said to me, "These are the ones who come out of the great tribulation, and washed their robes and made them white in the blood of the Lamb.

Here, John is witnessing the great multitude which no one could number, of all tribes, nations, peoples and tongues, having come out of the great tribulation but now standing before the throne and the Lamb, and yet the appearance of the dragon, beast and false prophet who cause these three and a half years of great tribulation against the Elect don't appear until Revelation 12 and 13. This kind of juxtaposition is typical of Revelation.

> *Because of the complexity of the vision John received, there is no simple way of writing everything down, other than the way he was instructed.*

The Book of Revelation contains both macro and micro views and perspectives, zooming in at times on specific details, whilst at others zooming out to give the big picture, like Revelation 12 which covers a much larger timeframe some of which is historical with the imagery of the birth and ascension of Jesus as the man-child snatched up to heaven. So, when reading Revelation 8:1,2 which gives the seventh seal in verse 1, and the start of the seven trumpets in verse 2, it's not enough to presume just because the reference to the trumpets comes after the reference to the seventh seal, they must therefore be one after the other chronologically. This is a key principle to have in our *'good student of the Word'* toolkit: that any separate sequence (or theme) given to John is chronological in itself, (for example, in the seven seals sequence, seal one is followed by seal two and so on), but when attempting to sort the sequences and themes together chronologically, the scripture reference should not be the only consideration.

> *For example, if you were asked to describe three weddings which had all taken place yesterday, the simplest way to do that is to describe them one after the other, but it doesn't mean they were sequential.*

Revelation 8:1 and 2 are connected grammatically by the use of the word *'And'*. *'And I saw the seven angels who were given seven trumpets.'* The use of *'And'* doesn't mean what's described in verse 2 follows that in verse 1. How else might John introduce the seven-trumpet sequence? Nowhere in Revelation does he try to teach, or give an apologetic to what he's witnessing, but he simply records as instructed. The use of *'And'* is perfectly acceptable in this case as the start of a new sequence. Indeed, numerous translations, don't use the word *'and'* but *'then'*.[104] The word *'and'* in the Greek can be

---

[104] The ESV, NET, RSV, CSB all translate the beginning of Revelation 8:2 as 'then I saw'

interpreted '*also*', in which case the translators could have written '*I also saw seven angels who were given seven trumpets*'. In summary then, because things have to be written sequentially, doesn't mean the events themselves are necessarily progressive. Therefore, just because the first reference to the seven trumpets in Revelation 8:2 follows the seventh seal in Revelation 8:1 does not disprove the proposition that the sixth seal and seventh trumpet converge on the Day of the Lord but is rather a literary necessity when describing multiple events, that one must follow the other in the text.

QB43 The Seals, Trumpets and Bowls (Part 2)

In our quest to determine where the sequences of seals, trumpets and bowls fit into the end-time narrative, I have laid an important chronological marker in stating that the sixth seal and seventh trumpet converge on the Day of the Lord when Jesus comes as the Son of Man to gather His Elect as in Matthew 24. I proposed in Quick Bite 41 the wrath of God will not yet have been unleashed up to this point. That's because the wrath of God is reserved until after the rapture and will be poured out in the seven bowls, which we'll come to later. We've dealt with objections to this position already from the progressive view in Quick Bite 42, but now we must respond to challenges from the simultaneous view, which believes the sequence of seals, trumpets and bowls are either concurrent or even describe the same event but from a different perspective, if that were so, then the bowls would not follow the trumpets but instead, as each sequence of seals and trumpets progressed, so would the seven bowls also[105].

---

[105] If that were the case, then the seven bowls of wrath would complete on the seventh trumpet which I have put forward as the day of the Lord. Now since I am proposing for the resurrection/rapture to also be at this time, the implications of the simultaneous view mean the elect would be upon the earth during the time of God's wrath being poured out, because the bowls are especially mentioned as bowls of wrath (we will cover this point later). That would be a major stumbling block in our eschatology since in passages like 1 Thessalonians 1:10 and 5:9 we are reassured we

The simultaneous view compares the details depicted in the three sequences and observes the similarities between them. For example, the first trumpet and first bowl both relate to the earth (Revelation 8:7, 16:2[106]), the second trumpet and second bowl relate to the sea (Revelation 8:8,9, 16:3[107]), the third trumpet and bowl relate to rivers and springs (Revelation 8:10,11, 16:4[108]), and the fourth trumpet and

---

shall not be subject to wrath. This seeming conflict is a major foundation stone in the pre-tribulation argument which proposes since we shall be delivered from the coming wrath the church will not be upon the earth during the great tribulation. However, the fundamental flaw in this view is that the great tribulation is not about the wrath of God, indeed, the point here is that the wrath of God (and of the Lamb) is withheld until the Day of the Lord at which point the redeemed are gathered safely after which the seven bowls of wrath are finally dispensed.

[106] The first angel sounded (trumpet): And hail and fire followed, mingled with blood, and they were thrown to the earth. And a third of the trees were burned up, and all green grass was burned up. (Revelation 8:7 NKJV).

So the first went and poured out his bowl upon the earth, and a foul and loathsome sore came upon the men who had the mark of the beast and those who worshiped his image. (Revelation 16:2 NKJV).

[107] Then the second angel sounded (trumpet): And something like a great mountain burning with fire was thrown into the sea, and a third of the sea became blood. And a third of the living creatures in the sea died, and a third of the ships were destroyed. (Revelation 8:8,9 NKJV).

Then the second angel poured out his bowl on the sea, and it became blood as of a dead man; and every living creature in the sea died. (Revelation 16:3 NKJV).

[108] Then the third angel sounded (trumpet): And a great star fell from heaven, burning like a torch, and it fell on a third of the rivers and on the springs of water. The name of the star is Wormwood. A third of the waters became wormwood, and many men died from the water, because it was made bitter. (Revelation 8:10,11 NKJV).

Then the third angel poured out his bowl on the rivers and springs of water, and they became blood. (Revelation 16:4 NKJV).

bowl both relate to the sun (Revelation 8:12, 16:8,9[109]). Now whilst the similarities are clearly observable, the resemblance is not enough to claim them as happening at the same time or indeed that they are even the same event. An example which undermines the reliability of the simultaneous view is the comparison of the earthquake mentioned in all three sequences, namely the sixth seal, the seventh trumpet and the seventh bowl. Listen carefully to the description of the earthquake in each.

12 I looked when He opened the sixth seal, and behold, there was a great earthquake; and the sun became black as sackcloth of hair, and the moon became like blood. 13 And the stars of heaven fell to the earth, as a fig tree drops its late figs when it is shaken by a mighty wind. 14 Then the sky receded as a scroll when it is rolled up, and every mountain and island was moved out of its place.
(Revelation 6:12-14 NKJV).

After the seventh trumpet we read:

19 Then the temple of God was opened in heaven, and the ark of His covenant was seen in His temple. And there were lightnings, noises, thunderings, an earthquake, and great hail.
(Revelation 11:19 NKJV).

---

[109] Then the fourth angel sounded (trumpet): And a third of the sun was struck, a third of the moon, and a third of the stars, so that a third of them were darkened. A third of the day did not shine, and likewise the night. (Revelation 8:12 NKJV).
Then the fourth angel poured out his bowl on the sun, and power was given to him to scorch men with fire. And men were scorched with great heat, and they blasphemed the name of God who has power over these plagues; and they did not repent and give Him glory. (Revelation 16:8,9 NKJV).

Then finally - 17 the seventh angel poured out his bowl into the air, and a loud voice came out of the temple of heaven, from the throne, saying, "It is done!" 18 And there were noises and thunderings and lightnings; and there was a great earthquake, such a mighty and great earthquake as had not occurred since men were on the earth. 19 Now the great city was divided into three parts, and the cities of the nations fell. And great Babylon was remembered before God, to give her the cup of the wine of the fierceness of His wrath. 20 Then every island fled away, and the mountains were not found. (Revelation 16:17-20 NKJV).

In each sequence there will be an earthquake. And because the devastation caused will be so great, especially with the sixth seal and seventh bowl earthquakes, the simultaneous view sees these as the same event, since such colossal damage can only happen once. The argument goes like this: '*If the sixth seal earthquake causes every mountain and island to be removed, then that's a final, unrepeatable process. The earthquake in Revelation 16:20 which records every island to flee away and every mountain to not be found must therefore be describing the same event.*' On the face of it, that would seem to be a good point. However, as always, let's go back to the text and see what it's actually saying and what it's not. Here's the sixth seal earthquake again in Revelation 6:14:

Then the sky receded as a scroll when it is rolled up, and every mountain and island was moved out of its place.

The Greek word for '*moved*' is '*kinéō*' (ke-neh-o) and means to be moved, set in motion, to remove. It also means: to excite, disturb, to throw into commotion, or to wag. Wag meaning to shake back and forth as in a dog wagging its tail. This word '*kinéō*' (ke-neh-o) is used to describe the riot of the Ephesians against Paul's preaching in Acts 21:30 which reads:

And all the city was disturbed (*'kinéō'*) other translations The whole city was rocked (*'kinéō'*) or Then all the city was stirred up (*'kinéō'*).

I suggest what Revelation 6:14 is describing in the sixth seal is not a disappearance or removal, but a shaking of the mountains as one would expect with an earthquake, but what it isn't describing is a complete disappearance as in the earthquake at the time of the seventh bowl in Revelation 16:20 which reads:

Then every island fled away, and the mountains were not found.

Incidentally, the word *'fled'* here in this verse in Greek means *'to escape safely out of danger, to shun something abhorrent, to flee, seek safety by flight'*. But what isn't in this verse is the word *'kinéō'* (ke-neh-o) as it was in Revelation 6:14.

In summary then, I have proposed the seventh trumpet and the sixth seal converge on the day of the Lord when the Lord will come on the clouds as the Son of Man with His angels to gather His Elect. The wrath of God has been withheld until this point as we learnt in Quick Bite 41, and as I will cover next time, the wrath of God is poured out in the seven bowls. Since this viewpoint does not conform to either the progressive or simultaneous view, I have responded to objections proposed by both. Now that we have done so I can confidently continue laying out this Bridal perspective on the unfolding of future events.

QB44 The Seals, Trumpets and Bowls (Part 3)

9 When He opened the fifth seal, I saw under the altar the souls of those who had been slain for the word of God and for the testimony which they held. 10 And they cried with a loud voice, saying, "How long, O Lord, holy and true, until You judge and avenge our blood on those who dwell on the earth?" 11 Then a white robe was given to each of them; and it was said to them that they should rest a little while longer[110], until both the number of their fellow servants and their brethren, who would be killed as they were, was completed. (Revelation 6:9-11 NKJV).

The great tribulation of the Elect will be a time of much suffering, persecution and as John saw in the opening of the fifth seal, even martyrdom for the saints of God. Those slain cry out asking *"How long O Lord until you avenge our blood?"* and they are told *"a little while longer until the number of those who would be killed was complete"*. The word for *'avenge'* in the Greek as in *'avenge our blood'* is the word *'ekdikéō'*, (ek-de-keh-o) and is found in Romans 12:19 NKJV:

---

[110] The vengeance of God has not yet come, since they are told to rest a little longer. Another indication that the wrath of God comes after the great tribulation.

19 Beloved, do not avenge yourselves, but rather give place to wrath; for it is written, "Vengeance is Mine, I will repay," says the Lord.

Here we see the connection between vengeance and wrath. How will the Lord avenge His righteous ones? Through wrath. He will repay, but as those under the altar in the fifth seal were informed, even though it would not be long, the time of wrath had not yet come. It is on the opening of the sixth seal - on the Day of the Lord, where we read Revelation 6:17:

the great day of his wrath is come; and who shall be able to stand?

This will mark the end of 1260 days of great tribulation and will initiate the sequence of seven bowls of wrath we find recorded in Revelation 16. Significantly before this in Revelation 14 and 15 we see the Elect, already gathered and in Heaven. The outpouring of God's wrath will never be upon His Bride, how can that be? Then Revelation 17,18 describes the judgement of '*Mystery Babylon the Great, the Mother of Harlots and Abominations of the Earth*' when the appeal of those slain and under the altar in Revelation 6 is answered. Revelation 19:2 NKJV reads:

For true and righteous are His judgments, because He has judged the great harlot who corrupted the earth with her fornication; and He has avenged on her the blood of His servants shed by her.

The day of wrath coming upon the earth will be an entirely righteous indignation from a God who is entirely holy. Sin will run its full course, and wickedness will flourish, as lawlessness runs rampant to replace the righteousness of God, with a toxic humanism and perversion of the created order. Yet even as in Noah's day, there will be opportunity to repent right up until the final hour.

Then I saw another angel flying in mid-air, and he had the eternal gospel to proclaim to those who live on the earth—to every nation, tribe, language and people. 7 He said in a loud voice, "Fear God and give him glory, because the hour of his judgment has come. Worship him who made the heavens, the earth, the sea and the springs of water."
(Revelation 14:6 NIV).

But for those who receive the mark of the beast, their fate is clear.

A third angel followed them and said in a loud voice: "If anyone worships the beast and its image and receives its mark on their forehead or on their hand, 10 they, too, will drink the wine of God's fury, which has been poured full strength into the cup of his wrath. They will be tormented with burning sulphur in the presence of the holy angels and of the Lamb. 11 And the smoke of their torment will rise for ever and ever. There will be no rest day or night for those who worship the beast and its image, or for anyone who receives the mark of its name." 12 This calls for patient endurance on the part of the people of God who keep his commands and remain faithful to Jesus. (Revelation 14:9 NIV).

Our God is a loving God! He is so merciful not treating us as our sins deserve that whilst we were still sinners He gave His only begotten Son, that whoever believes on Him will not perish but receive everlasting life. As Peter writes in 2 Peter 3:4 there are those who question the Day of the Lord saying:

Where is the promise of His coming? Things have not changed but continue to be as they always have been (my paraphrase).

Peter responds in verse 9 saying:

The Lord is not slow to fulfil his promise as some count slowness, but is patient toward you, not wishing that any should perish, but that all should reach repentance. [ESV]

To those who receive the gift of His Son Jesus, to those who have been washed in His blood and their sin expunged from the record, they will never be taken from His hand. To those who keep their lamps lit during the night vigil, who live a life worthy of the calling, who are numbered amongst the Elect they may be comforted the Lord has not forgotten them and will soon come for them to take them to the wedding of the Lamb. But there must be a day of reckoning. Sin must be dealt with once and for all. The reign of darkness imposed by the fallen minions of every demonic kind, rulers and authorities in the heavenly realms, will be torn from their thrones and stripped of their authority forever. We can endure the night because we know rejoicing will come in the morning. What a day it will be when the summation of all history will converge at that time. When the prophetic timeline of Jew and Gentile shall be joined forever when our Bridegroom shall see the travail of His soul and be satisfied when the longing of His heart to gather Jerusalem as a hen gathers her chicks shall finally be fulfilled. Those days shall soon be upon us, let us be comforted by Paul's words in Romans 5:9 ESV:

Since, therefore, we have now been justified by his blood, much more shall we be saved by him from the wrath of God.

QB45 The Transition of Kingdoms in 30 Days (Part 1)

15 Then the seventh angel sounded: And there were loud voices in heaven, saying, "The kingdoms of this world have become the kingdoms of our Lord and of His Christ, and He shall reign forever and ever!" 16 And the twenty-four elders who sat before God on their thrones fell on their faces and worshiped God, 17 saying: "We give You thanks, O Lord God Almighty, The One who is and who was and who is to come, Because You have taken Your great power and reigned. 18 The nations were angry, and Your wrath has come, And the time of the dead, that they should be judged, And that You should reward Your servants the prophets and the saints, And those who fear Your name, small and great, And should destroy those who destroy the earth." 19 Then the temple of God was opened in heaven, and the ark of His covenant was seen in His temple. And there were lightnings, noises, thunderings, an earthquake, and great hail. (Revelation 11:15-19 NKJV).

When the seventh trumpet is blown it will be accompanied with loud voices in heaven saying:

The kingdoms of this world have become the kingdoms of our Lord and of His Christ, and He shall reign forever and ever!

This climactic moment, this Day of the Lord will be like a line drawn in the sand marking the end of the age as we know it. This day will be on the opening of the sixth seal which we find recorded for us in Revelation 6:12-17, which ends saying:

For the day of His wrath has come, and who is able to stand.

This is the day the prophet Joel spoke of when the sun will be darkened and the moon become like blood, and Jesus taught us in Matthew 24:29-31 on that day *'His elect'* will be gathered. The Day of the Lord will mark the transition from one kingdom to another, from the Dominion of Darkness to the Dominion of Light. It will be no uncertain apocalypse or unveiling, yet there will still be much to take place before the final transition is complete. This is a good time to take a quick pause, reflect, revise and introduce the subject of future Quick Bites. So, first of all, let's be clear on what will take place on the Day of the Lord when Jesus returns as the Son of Man as in Matthew 24:

1.   The Great Gathering.

Let both grow together until the harvest, and at the time of harvest I will say to the reapers, "First gather together the tares and bind them in bundles to burn them, but gather the wheat into my barn." (Matthew 13:30).

There is one harvest for both the righteous and the unrighteous, when Jesus returns it will be a time of gathering for both. Jesus teaches this harvest will be at the end of the age, that's not the end of the world, but the end of this current era, as is Matthew 28:20 where He says:

Lo, I am with you always, even to the end of the age.

Unless you change the context of this parable into something else other than the world[111] and the end of the age, in my opinion, it's impossible to support a pre-trib position from this parable.[112]

2.   The Dead in Christ will be resurrected with a glorious new body.

51 Behold, I tell you a mystery: We shall not all sleep, but we shall all be changed-- 52 in a moment, in the twinkling of an eye, at the last trumpet. For the trumpet will sound, and the dead will be raised incorruptible, and we shall be changed. (1 Corinthians 15:51-52 NKJV).

3.   Those who have their garments washed in the blood of the Lamb, who have oil in their lamps upon His arrival shall be caught up to meet the Lord in the air when He comes.

15 For this we say to you by the word of the Lord, that we who are alive and remain until the coming of the Lord will by no means precede those who are asleep. 16 For the Lord Himself will descend from heaven with a shout, with the voice of an archangel, and with the trumpet of God. And the dead in Christ will rise first. 17 Then we who are alive and

---

[111] Later in Matthew 13:38 Jesus tells us exactly what the symbols in the parable mean. Here's what he tells His disciples "The field is the world, the good seeds are the sons of the kingdom, but the tares are the sons of the wicked one."

[112] There is a diversity of opinion and interpretation in the parable of the Wheat and Tares. I won't go into those here, only to point out the obvious which is so often overlooked, that however you interpret this parable, Jesus Himself clarified the underlying message when asked later by His disciples in Matthew 13:36. He made it clear that there was one harvest which would be at the end of the age and there was not a separate harvest for the righteous and the unrighteous. This point was further illustrated a few verses later in the parable of the dragnet Matthew 13:47-50 which teaches the separation of the righteous from the unrighteous is at the end of the age.

remain shall be caught up together with them in the clouds to meet the Lord in the air. And thus we shall always be with the Lord. (1 Thessalonians 4:15-17 NKJV).

4. The Great Tribulation will be over. [113]

29 Immediately after the tribulation of those days the sun will be darkened, and the moon will not give its light; the stars will fall from heaven, and the powers of the heavens will be shaken. (Matthew 24:29 NKJV).

5. The authority of the Beast will end.

And he was given a mouth speaking great things and blasphemies, and he was given authority to continue for forty-two months. [114] (Revelation 13:5 NKJV).

6. The trampling of the Holy City will end.

But leave out the court which is outside the temple, and do not measure it, for it has been given to the Gentiles. And they will tread the holy city underfoot for forty-two months. (Revelation 11:2 NKJV).

7. The seven bowls of wrath are about to be poured out. [115]

1 Then I heard a loud voice from the temple saying to the seven angels, "Go and pour out the bowls of the wrath of God on the earth."
(Revelation 16:1 NKJV).

---

[113] That is not to say the woes of man have ended but rather the time of trouble for the elect has stopped. Indeed, the distress of man is about to increase beyond comprehension.

[114] Forty-two months is the same as 1260 days which is the same as 'times, time and half a time' or three and half years.

[115] See Quick Bites 40 – 44 for more on the wrath of God.

8.   The time of the woman in the wilderness will be over.

But the woman was given two wings of a great eagle, that she might fly into the wilderness to her place, where she is nourished for a time and times and half a time, from the presence of the serpent. (Revelation 12: 14 NKJV).

Remember all I am sharing here in this Quick Bites series, is from the Bridal paradigm. She will help us to understand how everything connects together in one wonderful tapestry designed and intricately woven together by the Lord. We must keep our eye on the Lord of course, but also on the Bride, since she is what Creation is all about, the masterpiece of God. And she is becoming ever clearer as the future unfolds. So where is the Bride now at this point in the apocalypse? Well, I'll tell you a great mystery: At this time, when Jesus returns as the Son of Man, I believe the Bride will be caught up to Heaven, but she will also be gathered upon the Earth! (I will cover this later in greater detail in Quick Bites 47 to 55, *The Second Exodus'*) That may sound contradictory until we remember the Bride is both Jew and Gentile. There will be those who have made their preparations and kept their lamps lit, but there will also be those amongst Israel who have not yet received their Messiah. She is the wife who is not yet prepared, For before her wedding day, all Israel must be saved. There can be no Bride and no wedding without her. Yet when Jesus returns, all Israel has not yet been saved. She is still dispersed, under siege, and in need of a deliverer. Where will this deliverer come from? Paul quotes Isaiah when he writes:

and so all Israel will be saved, just as it is written, "The deliverer will come out of Zion; he will turn away ungodliness from Jacob." (Romans 11:26 LEB).

QB46 The Transition of Kingdoms in 30 Days (Part 2)

22 Then He said to the disciples, "The days will come when you will desire to see one of the days of the Son of Man, and you will not see it." (Luke 17:22 NKJV).

Though Jesus spoke these words to His disciples, I believe this verse can also be applied to Israel. When Jesus spoke these words, which is part of a larger discourse on the Second Coming in Luke's Gospel, He was already with Israel as the Son of Man, His atoning work of redemption and salvation, His ministry to the *'Lost Sheep of Israel'*, was all as the Son of Man, given to them as the Lamb of God. Yet it was those who were not a people, those who were from another *'sheep-fold'*, that entered in first through the Door of Salvation[116]. Israel as a whole had missed the days of the Son of Man, John writes:

He came to His own, and His own did not receive Him. (John 1:11 NKJV).

Luke writes:

14 But his citizens hated him, and sent a delegation after him, saying, "We will not have this man to reign over us." (Luke 19:14 NKJV).

---

[116] This is a broad stroke because many Jews were saved and healed when Jesus was among them, but mostly Israel rejected their Messiah on His first coming.

Yet Ezekiel writes:

33 "As I live," says the Lord GOD, "surely with a mighty hand, with an outstretched arm, and with fury poured out, I will rule over you."
(Ezekiel 20:33 NKJV).

In Luke 17:22 Jesus prophesies of a time in the future time when there will be a change of heart, and there will be a great longing to see Him again. This Jesus calls the *'days of the Son of Man'*. Just as He had been with them before, they would look back upon that time and covet for those days again. That day will come, though not at first, but after the tribulation of those days, Jesus will return as recorded in Matthew 24:29-31 as the Son of Man. Remember in Quick Bites 31 and 32, I shared how this coming was not the same as the Revelation 19 passage where we read Jesus returning not as a Son of Man, but as King of Kings and Lord of Lords. That's because in Matthew 24 He's coming for His Bride, but in Revelation 19 He's coming with His Bride. In Revelation 19:7 we read:

the wife has made herself ready,

this necessitates the salvation of both Jew and Gentile - the One New Man. For the salvation of Israel, Jesus will come again as the Son of Man. This is her moment.

37 O Jerusalem, Jerusalem, the one who kills the prophets and stones those who are sent to her! How often I wanted to gather your children together, as a hen gathers her chicks under her wings, but you were not willing! 38 See! Your house is left to you desolate; 39 for I say to you, you shall see Me no more till you say, "Blessed is He who comes in the name of the LORD!" (Matthew 23:37-39 NKJV).

Jesus wept over Jerusalem and longed to gather her to Himself. That day is coming soon. Even though we talk of gathering, this is more than geographical relocation, more than moving from one place to another, or even one dimension to another. This is not so much positional gathering but relational gathering! It isn't so much about gathering Israel geographically but gathering her into a personal and loving relationship with the Lord as her husband. He is coming for Israel once more as the Son of Man, and her song will be '*Blessed is He who comes in the name of the Lord*'.

> **What I am proposing here is that there will be a time after the rapture of those who are saved at His coming in Matthew 24, in which Jesus will be upon the earth as the Son of Man.**

It will be a time like no other time which has ever existed or ever shall again. It will be for the salvation of Lost Israel. He will gather her to Himself, but not even in the land of Israel at first. For there will be a second Exodus, just like Moses who foreshadowed Jesus, leading Israel out into the Wilderness, so Jesus will lead His people out into the Wilderness also. I will teach on these things later, but for now I'm making the point there will be a period of time, between Jesus' coming in Matthew 24 as the Son of Man and His coming in Revelation 19 as the King of Kings and Lord of Lords, in which lost Israel will be saved and gathered. Not just a geographical gathering to the Land of Israel, but a personal gathering unto the Lord. Israel will be gathered as a Bride to her Husband, and she will be in Heaven just in time for the Marriage of the Lamb. She will be the wife who has made herself ready. How long will this time be when Jesus is physically upon the earth to bring salvation to Israel and lead her back to Zion? Well, to answer that we need to understand a little more about the demise and destruction of the Beast.

As we have already seen, the authority of the Beast will be for forty-two months[117], which is 1260 days. But this doesn't mean the end of the Beast has come just yet. Yes, after 1260 days of great tribulation Jesus will return as the Son of Man, but it's not until Revelation 19:20 when Jesus returns as *'King of Kings and Lord of Lords'* when the Beast and False Prophet are cast alive into the Lake of Fire. This means that for a time they are still on the earth during the future *'days of the Son of Man'*. Though they won't have the same authority they had been given previously, they will be given other authority from another source:

12 The ten horns which you saw are ten kings who have received no kingdom as yet, but they receive authority for one hour as kings with the beast. 13 These are of one mind, and they will give their power and authority to the beast. (Revelation 17:12-13 NKJV).

In the following verse, notice how the focus has shifted away from the destruction of Jerusalem and Israel. Since Jesus is bodily upon the earth for this period as the Son of Man, the Lamb of God, He now becomes the focus of Satan's aggression.

14 These will make war with the Lamb, and the Lamb will overcome them, for He is Lord of lords and King of kings; and those who are with Him are called, chosen, and faithful. (Revelation 17:14 NKJV).

How long will this period last? Well, it is the time it takes between the removal of the Beast's authority which is to last for 1260 days,

---

[117] And he was given a mouth speaking great things and blasphemies, and he was given authority to continue for forty-two months. (Revelation 13:5 NKJV).

to the time when He is finally removed as the abomination that causes desolation. How long this will be we are told in Daniel 12:11 NKJV – which reads:

And from the time that the daily sacrifice is taken away, and the abomination of desolation is set up, there shall be one thousand two hundred and ninety days.

Daniel is told the abomination of desolation will be set up for 1290 days. For this reason, I believe the period of time between Jesus coming as the Son of Man in Matthew 24 and His coming as the King of Kings and Lord of Lords in Revelation 19 will be the difference between 1260 and 1290 days, which is thirty days. Thirty days during which the bowls of wrath will be poured out, thirty days during which Mystery Babylon will be destroyed, thirty days during which all Israel will be saved[118], and thirty days the transition in which the Kingdoms of this World become the Kingdoms of our God and His Christ.

---

[118] That is not to say it will take all thirty days for the salvation of Israel, but it will be during that time. To be more precise, I believe it will be ten days for Israel to come into the fulness of the New Covenant made with her. As I will show later, my belief is the Lord will return on the Feast of Trumpets which will initiate ten days of awe and repentance, leading up to Yom Kippur, the Day of Atonement.

QB47 The Second Exodus (Part 1)

A day of the LORD is about to come when your possessions will be divided as plunder in your midst. 2 For I will gather all the nations against Jerusalem to wage war; the city will be taken, its houses plundered, and the women raped. Then half of the city will go into exile, but the remainder of the people will not be taken away. 3 Then the LORD will go to battle and fight against those nations, just as he fought battles in ancient days. 4 On that day his feet will stand on the Mount of Olives which lies to the east of Jerusalem, and the Mount of Olives will be split in half from east to west, leaving a great valley. Half the mountain will move northward and the other half southward. 5 Then you will escape through my mountain valley, for the valley of the mountains will extend to Azal. Indeed, you will flee as you fled from the earthquake in the days of King Uzziah of Judah. Then the LORD my God will come with all his holy ones with him.
(Zechariah 14:1-5 NET).

When we talk of the gathering of the Elect it is not quite as simple as a singular rapture into the clouds in some sort of escapist theology. No, the truth is far more engaging, more gritty than this, much closer to home with troubling implications for both Jew and Gentile! Any eschatological perspective we adopt must be comprehensive, and it must be rooted in the Covenant promises God made to Israel.

> *The promise of gathering is made to her, the promise of resurrection is made to her, the promise of reigning forever is made to her.*

The church by no means replaces Israel, but then neither does Israel replace the church. If the truth be told, there will be neither Jew nor Gentile, but by virtue of belonging to Christ then we are all heirs of Abraham[119]. That doesn't mean, we will lose our ethnicity. In the same way, when Paul teaches there will not be male or female, doesn't mean we will lose our gender, that's not the point here. The principle is how the basis of our relationship with each other and with the Lord is not about any earthly, physical or human trait, but about our spiritual re-creation, *'flesh of His flesh, and bone of His bone'*, the Bride, the corporate expression of the Body of Christ, made of living stones.

On the Day of the Lord, the Elect will be gathered. As we have seen previously, this does include a rapture; a being caught up together in the clouds to meet the Lord in the air when He comes as the Son of Man, but along with those resurrected, this rapture into the air will only include those who are saved and ready for His coming. At this time, not all Israel is saved, and therefore the Bride will be in Heaven but also upon the earth. The Bride is not quite ready, not until Revelation 19:7 are we told the wife has made herself ready. Indeed, at the moment of the Lord's return in Matthew 24, Jerusalem will be

---

[119] There is neither Jew nor Greek, there is neither slave nor free, there is no male and female, for you are all one in Christ Jesus. And if you are Christ's, then you are Abraham's offspring, heirs according to promise. (Galatians 3:28-29 ESV),

in great distress, and though there is the current ongoing return of Jews back to their homeland today, we are told the tribes of Israel will still be dispersed around the world on the Day of the Lord. Speaking of the Day of the Lord listen to what Isaiah writes:

In that day[120] the root of Jesse, who shall stand as a signal for the peoples—of him shall the nations inquire, and his resting place shall be glorious. 11 In that day the Lord will extend his hand yet a second time to recover the remnant that remains of his people, from Assyria, from Egypt, from Pathros, from Cush, from Elam, from Shinar, from Hamath, and from the coastlands of the sea. 12 He will raise a signal for the nations and will assemble the banished of Israel, and gather the dispersed of Judah from the four corners of the earth. (Isaiah 11:10-12 ESV).

So let's pick up the story and look at what Zechariah wrote in chapter 14. He describes the siege of Jerusalem, when all the nations are gathered against her to make war. There will be great pillage, rape and exile of half the city, the Septuagint puts half the city will go into captivity. No wonder the Lord warns in Matthew 24:15-16 NKJV:

---

[120] The day referred to here is wonderfully depicted by Isaiah in the preceding verses 1-9 which is well worth reading. It clearly speaks of a day yet to come when 'the wolf shall dwell with the lamb and the leopard shall lie down with the young goat' v6a, a day when the 'earth shall be filled with the knowledge of the Lord as the waters cover the sea' v9b. But it is also a day when 'he shall strike the earth will the rod of his mouth and with the breath of his lips he shall kill the wicked' v4b. We might readily conclude this is the 'Day of the Lord'. In fact, the term 'In that day' or 'On that day' is repeated throughout the prophetic books of the Old Testament as usually referring to the 'Day of the Lord'. The point I am making therefore is that the tribes of Israel will still be dispersed when the Lord first returns.

15 Therefore when you see the 'abomination of desolation,' spoken of by Daniel the prophet, standing in the holy place (whoever reads, let him understand), 16 then let those who are in Judea flee to the mountains.

Zechariah then follows with the emphatic declaration of the Lord's return as a warrior to fight against those nations.

Then the LORD will go to battle and fight against those nations, just as he fought battles in ancient days. (Zechariah 14:3 NET).

But there are significant differences in the battle described here in Zechariah 14, from the Battle of Armageddon described in Revelation 19. In Revelation 19, there is no need for escape from the armies who wage war against the Lamb or from the Beast, on that occasion the Lord's victory will be decisive and complete. There is no suggestion of any other outcome except to conquer and defeat all those who dare to oppose the King of Kings and Lord of Lords. Here in Zechariah 14, there is no account of the finality found in Revelation 19, instead we are told the Lord will provide a means of escape for His people by standing on the Mount of Olives. The Mountain will split into two and a passage of escape, a great valley of the mountains will extend to Azal. Just as they had escaped before in the days of King Uzziah[121], Israel shall do so again. And just as

---

[121] The words of Amos, who was among the sheep breeders of Tekoa, which he saw concerning Israel in the days of Uzziah king of Judah, and in the days of Jeroboam the son of Joash, king of Israel, two years before the earthquake. (Amos 1:1 NKJV).
According to Josephus, this happened when King Uzziah was struck with leprosy for invading the priest's office; 'a great earthquake shook the ground, and a rent was made in the temple, and the bright rays of the sun shone through it; and fell upon the King's face; insomuch that the leprosy

the waters of the Red Sea had been parted to provide a means of escape for Israel from Egypt, so also the Lord will open the mountains to provide a valley in which to flee from her oppressors once more. When will this great Exodus take place? This has been a subject of great difficulty for Bible commentators for centuries, but now that we have firmly placed our chronological markers on our eschatological timeline, I believe it provides an opportunity to place this Exodus event with confidence also. To be continued.

---

seized upon him immediately. And before the city, at a place called Eroge, half the mountain broke off from the rest on the west' – Josephus, Antiquities of the Jews, Book IX 10:4.

QB48 The Second Exodus (Part 2)

In part one of this mini-series, I asked the question when will Jesus stand on the Mount of Olives to provide a means of escape for those besieged in Jerusalem? Let's read our core passage Zechariah 14:1-5 NET again:

A day of the LORD is about to come when your possessions will be divided as plunder in your midst. 2 For I will gather all the nations against Jerusalem to wage war; the city will be taken, its houses plundered, and the women raped. Then half of the city will go into exile, but the remainder of the people will not be taken away. 3 Then the LORD will go to battle and fight against those nations, just as he fought battles in ancient days. 4 On that day his feet will stand on the Mount of Olives which lies to the east of Jerusalem, and the Mount of Olives will be split in half from east to west, leaving a great valley. Half the mountain will move northward and the other half southward. 5 Then you will escape through my mountain valley, for the valley of the mountains will extend to Azal. Indeed, you will flee as you fled from the earthquake in the days of King Uzziah of Judah. Then[122] the LORD my God will come with all his holy ones[123] with him.

This passage clearly describes an end-time future event. Yet there are some very notable elements described by Zechariah which are not explicitly mentioned by either Jesus or the New Testament writers. Not least the Lord will stand on the Mount of Olives which will split in half to provide a means of escape for those besieged in Jerusalem[124]. This lack of reference poses a problem for the Bible student in understanding when this event will take place. Certainly, if one takes the view that Jesus returns only once, and therefore the Matthew 24 account of Jesus returning as the Son of Man on the clouds to gather His Elect is seen as the same event as Revelation 19 when Jesus returns out of heaven this time on a white horse, not as the Son of Man, but as the King of Kings and Lord of Lords, then there's a real conundrum here. If indeed there is just one return then we must also squeeze Zechariah's prophecy in chapter 14 into the

---

[122] The word 'then' is not found in the original manuscripts. This could be misleading, as the use of 'then' could suggest a subsequent action. Viz, the Lord will return with all his holy ones after the escape from Jerusalem at a later time. The New King James Version uses 'thus', better still the Hebrew Names Version omits 'then' entirely. To me it is a recapitulation of the preceding passage but with further emphasis; when the Lord returns and stands on the Mount of Olives, He will not be alone but will come with all his holy ones.

[123] The word here is qāḏôš (Stong's H6918) meaning holy ones. The use of 'holy ones' is interchangeable between the 'saints' and the 'angels', but in this case we are looking at Jesus returning with His angels.

[124] As incredible as it sounds, I have read one popular commentator who proposes this flight of Israel is from the Lord. I fail to comprehend that position on numerous grounds, not least the context of the passage itself which describes the inhabitants of Jerusalem under great peril from the nations of the world who are surrounding her. When the Lord returns, He will fight for her not against her. It is from the nations surrounding Jerusalem that those within her walls are in peril.

same time, but herein lies the problem: because Revelation 19 quite clearly teaches the Beast, False Prophet and armies coming against the Lord will meet a rather gruesome end and be totally annihilated, whereas in Zechariah 14 it is about flight and escape of those in Jerusalem from her oppressors. Here's how the battle is described in Revelation 19:17-21 NKJV:

17 Then I saw an angel standing in the sun; and he cried with a loud voice, saying to all the birds that fly in the midst of heaven, "Come and gather together for the supper of the great God, 18 that you may eat the flesh of kings, the flesh of captains, the flesh of mighty men, the flesh of horses and of those who sit on them, and the flesh of all people, free and slave, both small and great." 19 And I saw the beast, the kings of the earth, and their armies, gathered together to make war against Him who sat on the horse and against His army. 20 Then the beast was captured, and with him the false prophet who worked signs in his presence, by which he deceived those who received the mark of the beast and those who worshipped his image. These two were cast alive into the lake of fire burning with brimstone. 21 And the rest were killed with the sword which proceeded from the mouth of Him who sat on the horse. And all the birds were filled with their flesh.

Does this sound like the same event described by Zechariah? How would it be possible for the armies in Zechariah 14 to continue to hold Jerusalem under siege if they are about to be annihilated as Revelation 19 describes? The Zechariah 14 event is about escape, but the Lord's return in Revelation 19 is about vanquish. In my opinion it simply is not possible to reconcile what Zechariah prophesied in chapter 14 with the battle of Armageddon described in Revelation 19, and if that is so then we must accept a separate and earlier time of Jesus upon the earth. But it is not only the difference in the battles described which separate these two events from each other. For example, since in Revelation 19 Jesus is returning with His Bride, how is it Israel is still upon the earth and in need of a deliverer as in Zechariah 14? If Israel were saved at this point, she would not need a horizontal means of escape out of Jerusalem, because she would receive a vertical gathering up to meet the Lord coming on the clouds. Interesting. Does it mean she missed the wedding of the Lamb? I don't think so! This can never be since the Wife who has made herself ready is inclusive of Israel. The wedding contract is made with her. Only by virtue of being grafted into the Olive Tree is the Gentile church able to participate in the covenant blessings and promises made to Israel. This is our position at Call2Come: we have prioritised the Bride as the central thread, the foundational piece in which there is no negotiation.

There is one Bride and one wedding. And since when Jesus returns to judge and make war in Revelation 19, He will be accompanied by His Bride, it necessitates an earlier occasion in which Israel will be saved, and for her salvation, Jesus will come again as the Son of Man. This means Jesus upon the earth before Revelation 19, in other words, when Jesus returns as the King of Kings and Lord of Lords it will not be the first time He would have returned.

Zechariah's prophecy helps us to clearly identify an earlier time of Jesus upon the earth. Now this eschatological viewpoint simply isn't possible when holding to a one return of Jesus position, which leaves us with a choice: We either leave Israel out of the picture, and consider her grafted into the Bride later, during the Millennium once Jesus has returned, or we put things in order, accept the marriage covenant is made with Israel, accept that it is the Gentiles who are grafted into her, and accept that when Revelation 19:7 says *'the wife has made herself ready'* that it means Israel. This still leaves us with the question: When will Jesus stand on the Mount of Olives? When will the Second Exodus begin?

QB49 The Second Exodus (Part 3)

When asked by His disciples what would be the sign of His coming and of the end of the age,[125] we have no record of Jesus mentioning the escape through the Mount of Olives foreseen by the prophet Zechariah. The signs He gives are varied but does not include this particular part of Zechariah's prophecy. If Jesus were to stand on the Mount of Olives before His return as the Son of Man in Matthew 24, surely He would have mentioned this amongst the signs He gave to mark that great day. So when will Zechariah's prophecy in chapter 14 take place? I believe it will be when Jesus returns in Matthew 24, for He will not allow His people to suffer one more day than those already ascribed.[126] Those number of days is unequivocally given as 1260[127], the second half of Daniel's seventieth week [128]. Jesus said immediately after the tribulation of those days, He would come as the Son of Man upon the clouds of heaven with power and great glory[129]. And Hebrews

---

[125] Matthew 24:3.

[126] Since it cannot be before or after the return of Matthew 24, then we must conclude it is one of the same. Zechariah 14:5 records the Lord returning with His holy ones, which parallels Matthew 24:30,31.

[127] Daniel 12:7.

[128] Daniel 9:20-27.

[129] There is congruence here between the two passages of Zechariah 14:1-5 and Matthew 24 for both passages describe a return of the Lord accompanied by the angels. Furthermore, we know Daniel was informed the time of Israel's trouble would last for three and half years, which is also the duration of the great tribulation after which Jesus returns.

9:38 tells us He will bring salvation with Him when He comes. This salvation is two-fold. It will complete the salvation of those who are His and *'eagerly await His appearing'*[130], but it will also be for the salvation of Israel who have yet to enter into the New Covenant relationship with Him. The return of Jesus in Matthew 24 will fulfil more than one promise and will serve to bring convergence between two prophetic timelines, namely that of both Jew and Gentile back together into one-fold, one Elect, one New Man, one Bride. The partial hardening of Israel Paul writes of in Romans 11:25 shall be ended, and the day of their salvation shall come. This is a key point for us to understand.

> *What I am saying is when Jesus comes as the Son of Man upon the clouds with great glory, it will not be as simple as we might have previously assumed, for there is still much to transpire.*

On the great day of the Lord, He is coming for His Bride, even though at that time His Bride will not yet be fully complete or ready. Yes, of course, there will be those of us who are ready and prepared, and if so, then as promised we shall be caught up together with the resurrected saints, to meet the Lord in the air when He comes[131], but the Wife will not yet be ready, because Israel will not yet be fully saved and therefore the wedding of the Lamb will not yet have come. There can be no wedding without Israel, because the promise is made to her and there is but one wife, the One New Man. When Jesus returns at first in Matthew 24, He will do so as the Son of Man, because there is still an appointed time for Israel in which she shall be saved. For a brief period, the Bride will be in Heaven and also

---

[130] 2 Timothy 4:8.
[131] 1 Thessalonians 4:17.

upon the earth. Those who are ready for His return will now be in Heaven, but Israel will still be upon the earth, and Jesus will be with her upon the earth to lead her back to Mount Zion in time for the Wedding, just like Moses led Israel through the wilderness to Mount Sinai to enter into a marital covenant with the Lord. Don't worry, I'll cover these points later in this series.

I've presented a very different picture to the popular conception of the Lord turning around to return to Heaven for His marriage with those who have just been gathered up. That would mean a wedding without Israel, how can that be? Remember one of the key principles I've been teaching throughout all these Quick Bites, is the Bride is central to our understanding and interpretation of how end-time events will unfold. We need to think Bridal. Where is the Bride at any point in the text? This means keeping our eye on Israel all the time because the covenant is made with her. Jesus' role as Saviour, as the Son of Man, as the Lamb of God, is not yet complete. Israel rejected Him on His first coming, but this will not be the case on His second coming. For at that time, Zechariah writes in chapter 12:10 the Lord:

will pour out on the house of David and the inhabitants of Jerusalem a spirit of grace and pleas for mercy, so that, when they look on me, on him whom they have pierced, they shall mourn for him, as one mourns for an only child, and weep bitterly over him, as one weeps over a firstborn. [ESV]

When Jesus comes as the Son of Man on the clouds, He will indeed gather His Elect. But as we have seen in Quick Bite 36 – 38, the Elect is inclusive of Israel but not exclusive to her. The Elect are the *'Eklektos'*, the chosen, the Bride. Yes, there will be a gathering up to meet the Lord in the air and Jesus will present us to the Father[132] at that time, but He will not remain in Heaven, instead, He will continue His journey to Earth and gather together the rest of His Elect, the rest of His Bride. Jesus will bring deliverance for Israel by standing on the Mount of Olives exactly after the allotted 1260 days and not a day more. Israel will not suffer beyond the number of those days under the persecution of the Beast or the nations who rage against her. Revelation 11:2 NKJV reads:

But leave out the court which is outside the temple, and do not measure it, for it has been given to the Gentiles. And they will tread the holy city underfoot for forty-two months.

Immediately after the number of those days is complete, the Lord will return but He will not be alone. The Prophet Joel writes of this moment in Joel 3:11 ESV:

Hasten and come, all you surrounding nations, and gather yourselves there. Bring down your warriors, O LORD.

Dear Jerusalem will suffer greatly, but the Lord will not abandon her forever[133]. Did you know the very name Zechariah means '*Yahweh remembers*'? And the Lord will indeed remember His people:

For Jacob is the Lord's inheritance. (Deuteronomy 32:9).

---

[132] because we know that the one who raised Jesus will also raise us together with Jesus and present us together with you. (2 Corinthians 4:14 LEB).
Now unto him that is able to keep you from falling, and to present you faultless before the presence of his glory with exceeding joy, (Jude 1:24 NKJV).
[133] For the LORD will not forsake His people, for His great name's sake, because it has pleased the LORD to make you His people. (1 Samuel 12:22 NKJV).

Isaiah writes:

14 But Zion said, "The LORD has forsaken me; my Lord has forgotten me." 15 Can a woman forget her nursing child, that she should have no compassion on the son of her womb? Even these may forget, yet I will not forget you. 16 Behold, I have engraved you on the palms of my hands; your walls are continually before me. (Isaiah 49:14-16 ESV).

It is here in Jerusalem, and specifically Mount Zion which will be forever the city of the great king. Here is what the psalmist writes in Psalm 48 [ESV]:

1 Great is the LORD and greatly to be praised in the city of our God! His holy mountain, 2 beautiful in elevation, is the joy of all the earth, Mount Zion, in the far north, the city of the great King. 3 Within her citadels God has made himself known as a fortress. 4 For behold, the kings assembled; they came on together. 5 As soon as they saw it, they were astounded; they were in panic; they took to flight. 6 Trembling took hold of them there, anguish as of a woman in labour. 7 By the east wind you shattered the ships of Tarshish. 8 As we have heard, so have we seen in the city of the LORD of hosts, in the city of our God, which God will establish forever. — Selah 9 We have thought on your steadfast love, O God, in the midst of your temple. 10 As your name, O God, so your praise reaches to the ends of the earth. Your right hand is filled with righteousness. 11 Let Mount Zion be glad! Let the daughters of Judah rejoice because of your judgments! 12 Walk about Zion, go around her, number her towers, 13 consider well her ramparts, go through her citadels, that you may tell the next generation

14 that this is God, our God forever and ever. He will guide us forever.

QB50 The Second Exodus (Part 4)

5 Then I, Daniel, looked, and behold, two others stood, one on this bank of the stream and one on that bank of the stream. 6 And someone said to the man clothed in linen, who was above the waters of the stream, "How long shall it be till the end of these wonders?" 7 And I heard the man clothed in linen, who was above the waters of the stream; he raised his right hand and his left hand toward heaven and swore by him who lives forever that it would be for a time, times, and half a time, and that when the shattering of the power of the holy people comes to an end all these things would be finished. (Daniel 12:5-7 ESV).

As we have seen, there will be a time of unprecedented suffering to take place at the end of this age which is foretold in both the Old and New Testaments. There are many different names ascribed to this period of suffering or tribulation, but whatever term we use we are referring to the same three-and-a-half-year period, which is the second half of Daniel's seventieth week in Daniel 9:27[134], Jacob's trouble Jeremiah 30:7[135], or the great tribulation Matthew 24:21[136]. Though there will be a different agenda being played out for Israel and the Gentiles, it is still the same period of time.

And in our mini Quick Bite series '*The Second Exodus*', we are specifically focussed upon Israel and what the future holds for her. Remember to keep the Bride in full view, and ask, how will the Lord prepare His people Israel to be the wife who has made herself ready as in Revelation 19:7? That's the question, isn't it? Because that's the Lord's heart and desire, what all of Creation has been about; to prepare a Bride He will become one with as in a marriage relationship. As incredible as that sounds, what an awesome and unfathomable act of Divine Love and mercy it truly is. Who are we, that our Lord should be so mindful of us and loving? Yet this is the truth of the Gospel, the Divine Mystery being revealed. Let us therefore align our hearts with His, and make ourselves ready as His Bride, the wife of the Lamb.

Last time I shared how, for a brief period, the Bride would be both in Heaven and upon the earth, because when the Lord returns as the Son of Man, He is not only coming for His prepared Bride but for Israel also who has yet to enter into the New Covenant. Now those

---

[134] Then he shall confirm a covenant with many for one week; But in the middle of the week He shall bring an end to sacrifice and offering. And on the wing of abominations shall be one who makes desolate, Even until the consummation, which is determined, Is poured out on the desolate. (Daniel 9:27 NKJV).

[135] Alas! For that day is great, So that none is like it; And it is the time of Jacob's trouble, But he shall be saved out of it. (Jeremiah 30:7 NKJV).

[136] For then there will be great tribulation, such as has not been since the beginning of the world until this time, no, nor ever shall be. (Matthew 24:21 NKJV).

who are ready, prepared and waiting for the Lord's return, they shall be gathered into Heaven on that great Day of the Lord, but what of those in Israel who are not yet saved, where will they be, where will the unprepared wife be when Jesus returns? I believe there is a threefold answer to this question.

First, some of Israel will already have been in the wilderness for three and a half years.

But the woman was given the two wings of the great eagle so that she might fly from the serpent into the wilderness, to the place where she is to be nourished for a time, and times, and half a time. (Revelation 12:14 ESV).

But not all of Israel will leave their homeland or Jerusalem. Though Jesus had warned them to do so when they see the Abomination of Desolation, we find those who remained in Jerusalem now under attack from the nations of the world. Zechariah writes:

A day of the LORD is about to come when your possessions will be divided as plunder in your midst. 2 For I will gather all the nations against Jerusalem to wage war; the city will be taken, its houses plundered, and the women raped. Then half of the city will go into exile, but the remainder of the people will not be taken away (Zechariah 14:1-2 NET).

Then lastly, there will be a third group of people who are neither in Jerusalem nor the place in the wilderness provided for the woman. Here's Daniel 12:7 again, this time reading from the Septuagint:

And I heard the man clothed in linen, who was over the water of the river, and he lifted up his right hand and his left hand to heaven, and swore by him that lives for ever, that it should be for a time of times and half a time: when the dispersion is ended they shall know all these things.

Did you notice the reference to the dispersion? The dispersion will end after the time of Jacob's trouble, after the great tribulation. Now of course, we know since 1948 Israel has been politically recognised and many Jews have been returning to their homeland ever since, and I don't want to take anything away from this return back to Israel, but when looking at the Biblical references to the return of the dispersed tribes of Israel back to their homeland, then we cannot fail to notice the completion of this return is specifically prophesied as taking place on or after the Day of the Lord, which is after the great tribulation. Here are some more scriptures referring specifically to this gathering:

In that day the root of Jesse, who shall stand as a signal for the peoples—of him shall the nations inquire, and his resting place shall be glorious. 11 In that day the Lord will extend his hand yet a second time to recover the remnant that remains of his people, from Assyria, from Egypt, from Pathros, from Cush, from Elam, from Shinar, from Hamath, and from the coastlands of the sea. 12 He will raise a signal for the nations and will assemble the banished of Israel and gather the dispersed of Judah from the four corners of the earth. (Isaiah 11:10-12 ESV).

For thus says the Lord GOD: Behold, I, I myself will search for my sheep and will seek them out. 12 As a shepherd seeks out his flock when he is among his sheep that have been scattered, so will I seek out my sheep, and I will rescue them from all places where they have been scattered on a day of clouds and thick darkness. (Ezekiel 34:11,12 ESV).

7 "Alas! That day is so great there is none like it; it is a time of distress for Jacob; yet he shall be saved out of it. 8 And it shall come to pass in that day", declares the LORD of hosts, "that I will break his yoke from off your neck, and I will burst your bonds, and foreigners shall no more make a servant of him. 9 But they shall serve the LORD their God and David their king, whom I will raise up for them. 10 Then fear not, O Jacob my servant", declares the LORD, "nor be dismayed, O Israel; for behold, I will save you from far away, and your offspring from the land of their captivity. Jacob shall return and have quiet and ease, and none shall make him afraid." (Jeremiah 30:7-10 ESV).

What each of these verses tells us is that the gathering of the dispersed remnant of Israel will take place on a particular day, a specific time in the future. Ezekiel calls it *'a day of clouds and thick darkness'*, and Jeremiah describes it *'a time of distress for Jacob'*, when Israel shall be saved. It will be at that time, when David their King will be raised up, which is a Messianic reference to Jesus as the King.

QB51 The Second Exodus (Part 5)

he gathering of Israel was prophesied many times by the Old
Testament prophets, but more than this, the time of their
gathering is also foretold as connected with the Day of the
Lord. Let's take Zephaniah for example. Much of Zephaniah is
about the Day of the Lord, about a coming Judgement of Israel, a
gathering and punishment of nations, but the final verses end with
hope for Jerusalem and Israel.

Here's a quote from Zephaniah 3:14-20 [NKJV]:

14 Sing, O daughter of Zion! Shout, O Israel! Be glad and
rejoice with all your heart, O daughter of Jerusalem! 15 The
LORD has taken away your judgments, He has cast out your
enemy. The King of Israel, the LORD, is in your midst; You
shall see disaster no more. 16 In that day it shall be said to
Jerusalem: "Do not fear; Zion, let not your hands be weak. 17
The LORD your God in your midst, The Mighty One, will save;
He will rejoice over you with gladness, He will quiet you with
His love, He will rejoice over you with singing." 18 "I will
gather those who sorrow over the appointed assembly, who
are among you, To whom its reproach is a burden. 19 Behold,
at that time I will deal with all who afflict you; I will save
the lame, And gather those who were driven out; I will
appoint them for praise and fame In every land where they
were put to shame. 20 At that time I will bring you back,

Even at the time I gather you; For I will give you fame and praise Among all the peoples of the earth, When I return your captives before your eyes," Says the LORD.

Notice in this prophecy how the Lord the King of Israel will be among His people (verse 17). Interestingly Zephaniah specifically mentions Zion and writes, *'In that day it shall be said to Jerusalem: "Do not fear Zion, let not your hands be weak. The Lord your God in your midst, The Mighty One will save"'*. This is a picture of the Lord physically present amongst His people in Jerusalem to save them, He will be amongst them as the King of Israel, the Mighty One. Zephaniah writes the Lord will rejoice over Israel with gladness, quiet them with His love and rejoice over them with singing. At that time, the Lord will deal with all her oppressors and will save them. Could this be a reference to when Jerusalem will be delivered, at the time when the nations surround her? I believe so. He will stand upon the Mount of Olives and provide a means of escape. Notice this day of flight from Jerusalem is also the day of gathering for those dispersed elsewhere. Zephaniah prophesies, *'At that time, I will bring you back, even at the time I gather you'*.

Okay, a quick recap: I've been going through the events that will take place when the Lord returns in Matthew 24. In particular, our focus has been upon the Bride, and specifically how she will be the wife who has made herself ready in Revelation 19, because when Jesus returns in Matthew 24, the wife isn't yet ready, for Israel is not yet fully saved. Indeed, when Jesus returns as the Son of Man, Israel will be in great distress. But the Lord will come for her and not abandon her. There is a period of time, the days of the Son of Man, in which the Lord will lead Israel in the same way Moses led Israel out of Egypt, away from her oppressors, to bring her through the wilderness to Mount Sinai.

There are many similarities between the first exodus and the second exodus. In the first exodus just as the waters of the Red Sea were parted to provide a means of escape Exodus 14:21[137], so shall the Mount of Olives be parted in the second exodus for those in Jerusalem to flee Zechariah 14:4,5[138]. In the first Exodus the Lord bore His people on *'eagles' wings'* to bring them to himself Exodus 19:4[139], Israel will once again be carried upon the *'wings of a great eagle'* Revelation 12:14[140]. Or how about Ezekiel 20:10[HCSB] which reads:

So I brought them out of the land of Egypt and led them into the wilderness..

In the first Exodus, Israel escaped from her oppressors in Egypt, did you know that in the book of Revelation Jerusalem is referred to as Egypt[141]. Jerusalem is referred to symbolically as Sodom and Egypt,

---

[137] Then Moses stretched out his hand over the sea; and the LORD caused the sea to go back by a strong east wind all that night, and made the sea into dry land, and the waters were divided. (Exodus 14:21 NKJV).
[138] And in that day His feet will stand on the Mount of Olives, Which faces Jerusalem on the east. And the Mount of Olives shall be split in two, From east to west, Making a very large valley; Half of the mountain shall move toward the north And half of it toward the south. Then you shall flee through My mountain valley, For the mountain valley shall reach to Azal. Yes, you shall flee As you fled from the earthquake In the days of Uzziah king of Judah. Thus the LORD my God will come, And all the saints with You. (Zechariah 14:4,5 NKJV).
[139] You have seen what I did to the Egyptians, and how I bore you on eagles' wings and brought you to Myself. (Exodus 19:4 NKJV).
[140] But the woman was given two wings of a great eagle, that she might fly into the wilderness to her place, where she is nourished for a time and times and half a time, from the presence of the serpent. (Revelation 12:14 NKJV).
[141] And their dead bodies will lie in the street of the great city which spiritually is called Sodom and Egypt, where also our Lord was crucified. (Revelation 11:8 NKJV).

in both of those places there was an escape[142]! Moses led Israel out of Egypt, so also the Lord will lead Israel out of symbolic Egypt which is Jerusalem. Now, where was it they went after escaping through the Red Sea? It was into the Wilderness. Deuteronomy 8:2 explains the Lord led Israel into the wilderness to humble and to test them, to reveal what was in their heart and whether they would keep His commands or not. It was in the wilderness where Israel became the betrothed wife of Jehovah, with the marriage covenant established upon Mount Sinai. I hope to show how this same process will take place once more.

> *The Lord Jesus will be among His people, and He will lead them into the wilderness to test them, to sift them and to prepare them as the wife who has made herself ready. The wife will be prepared in the wilderness. This is always the case, the Bride in the Wilderness. When we speak of the gathering, it will not be to Jerusalem or even to Israel, not at first, but it will be into the wilderness.*

Here's what Ezekiel writes in chapter 20:33,34 [ESV]:

As I live, declares the Lord GOD, surely with a mighty hand and an outstretched arm and with wrath poured out I will be king over you. 34 I will bring you out from the peoples and gather you out of the countries where you are scattered, with a mighty hand and an outstretched arm, and with wrath poured out.

---

[142] In addition to being a place of escape and impending judgement, I believe there are other reasons why Jerusalem was spiritually connected with Sodom. It will be the subject of future Quick Bites but suffice to say here I believe Jerusalem will be at the pinnacle of her adultery during the three and a half years leading up to the Day of the Lord.

I have yet to mention the Feasts of the Lord but will now do so. Every feast has a prophetic fulfilment and is grouped into either the *'Spring Feasts'* or the *'Fall (Autumn) Feasts'*. Just as all the spring feasts were wonderfully fulfilled on Jesus' first coming, the fall feasts will be so on His second. On the prophetic calendar, the next feast is that of Yom Teruah, otherwise known as the Feast of Trumpets, and what I am teaching on the Second Exodus will be the fulfilment of the Feast of Trumpets, which initiates ten Days of Awe up to Yom Kippur the Day of Atonement[143]. All during these days of awe, the key emphasis is upon self-examination and repentance.

Now follow me closely here: In Quick Bites 40 – 44, a key point I brought out was how the wrath of God is reserved until the Day of the Lord. The sixth seal and seventh trumpet mark the Day of the Lord and the commencement of wrath. Because the Day of the Lord, will be upon the Feast of Trumpets, it means the ten days of awe, (during which will be the final opportunity for repentance and salvation of Israel), will also be a time of wrath upon the earth. That's what Ezekiel mentions here at the time of the gathering of Israel, the Lord will gather His people out of the countries where they are scattered with an outstretched arm and with wrath poured out[144]. Ezekiel continues in verses 35-37:

---

[143] Of course, there is the final Feast of Tabernacles but that will be once the 'Wife has made herself ready', and therefore after the Second Exodus. I will cover the Feast of Tabernacles in Quick Bite 60.

[144] I do not suggest here that the ten days of awe will be when the seven bowls of wrath will be poured out. I believe those judgements will only take place after Israel has been safely gathered in; not only gathered in upon the earth, but there will come a time when she will be gathered in and enter Heaven to join those waiting for her and singing the song that only the Bride can sing and only the redeemed can learn. We find this

35 And I will bring you into the wilderness of the peoples, and there I will enter into judgment with you face to face. 36 As I entered into judgment with your fathers in the wilderness of the land of Egypt, so I will enter into judgment with you, declares the Lord GOD. 37 I will make you pass under the rod, and I will bring you into the bond of the covenant. [ESV]

Wow, how amazing, the Lord makes the similarity between the first and second exoduses. He says, just as I judged your fathers in the wilderness, so I will do so with you. He also says He will enter into judgement with them face to face, that's because Jesus will be physically with them at that time. Where will this gathering take place? It is into the wilderness of the peoples, other translations say the wilderness of the nations, where this gathering will be. I will continue next time.

---

chronology in Revelation chapters fourteen to sixteen. Yet though the bowls are withheld at first does not mean there will not be wrath. Indeed, there will be great wrath from the outset. When the Lord goes forth and fights against the nations as He fights in the day of battle, He will do so with wrath.

QB52 The Second Exodus (Part 6)

Trying to locate where the gathering of Israel will be on the Day of the Lord is notoriously difficult, and I will do well not to be absolute in my study. Ezekiel 20:35 says '*I will bring you into the wilderness of the peoples (or nations)*', but we are not given any explicit reference to where this wilderness might be. So are there any other scriptures that do give an actual place name, or at least a connection with somewhere we might more readily identify? Well, our key passage in Zechariah 14 does say the valley of the mountains will reach to Azal, and those in Jerusalem will take this route as they flee. But this is still not enough, first because the location of Azal is disputed, and secondly, even though the flight of the refugees from Jerusalem will take this route, doesn't mean this is where they will finish their journey. So where else might we look? We are searching for a scripture that locates Jesus upon the earth with His people during the time of the gathering, which indicates where that location may be. Well, how about the prophet Micah?

12 I will surely assemble all of you, O Jacob, I will surely gather the remnant of Israel; I will put them together like sheep of the fold (Bozrah), Like a flock in the midst of their pasture; They shall make a loud noise because of so many people. 13 The one who breaks open will come up before them; They will break out, Pass through the gate, And go out by it; Their king will pass before them, With the LORD at their head. (Micah 2:12-13 NKJV).

I love this text, and yes it does tick several boxes. It is a reference to the gathering of the remnant of Israel, and it does place the Lord amongst His people. '*Their King will pass before them*', Micah writes, '*the Lord at their head.*' Hence this passage does qualify as fitting the time of the gathering with the Lord amongst His people. It does fit into our Second Exodus narrative. But what of location? Does this verse have a geographical reference that can help us identify where the gathering will be? Well, as I previously mentioned I will not state this as absolute or doctrinal, but as my belief and understanding when letting scripture interpret scripture, I believe there is enough to give a good indication of where the Lord will gather His people, and there is a clue right here in this text found in Micah. It's well buried under the translation process, but if you go back to the original Hebrew, the phrase '*sheep of the fold*' Micah 2:12 actually uses the word '*botsrah*', which although does mean sheepfold, it is also used to mean the place Bozrah which was a chief city of the ancient kingdom of Edom the homeland of Jacob's brother Esau. Here's the translation in the King James Version:

I will surely assemble, O Jacob, all of thee; I will surely gather the remnant of Israel; I will put them together as the sheep of Bozrah, as the flock in the midst of their fold: they shall make great noise by reason of the multitude of men. (Micah 2:12 KJV).

Scholars suggest Bozrah is in the mountain district of Petra about twenty miles southeast of the Dead Sea in the Land of Jordan today. Now that is interesting because there are other scriptures which refer to Edom and its capital Bozrah in the end times. The story of Israel and Edom goes right back to the story of Jacob and Esau. There had always been a rivalry between them, then over many generations the two brothers became the kingdoms of Israel and Edom, but the enmity between them continued. This enmity explains why Israel, having been delivered out of Egypt when travelling through the wilderness on their way to Canaan, were heavily opposed and denied entry by the Edomites to pass through their territory. Numbers 20:14-21[145] gives the account. It wasn't until after forty years of wandering around in the wilderness that Israel was finally permitted to pass through Edom territory Deuteronomy 2:2-8[146]. Could it be there was unfinished business with Edom? Certainly, the prophets suggest this. Even though the actual geopolitical kingdom of Edom was destroyed by the Babylonians in the sixth century BC, there is a sense in which the spirit of hostility towards Israel personified by Esau and Edom continues in the nations today.

By the rivers of Babylon, the psalmist laments over Zion, and writes:

Remember, O LORD, against the Edomites the day of Jerusalem, how they said, "Lay it bare, lay it bare, down to its foundations!" (Psalms 137:7 ESV).

What judgement there shall be indeed against those nations who shall seek the demise of Jerusalem and of Israel in the days to come. Will the Lord not deal with them like He did the Edomites of old? There are fascinating parallels here. Sadly, we don't have time to go into them all now, but how about this one: Whilst Israel was refused entry into Edom during the first exodus, it will be Bozrah in Edom,

---

[145] Then he said, "You shall not pass through." So Edom came out against them with many men and with a strong hand. Thus Edom refused to give Israel passage through his territory; so Israel turned away from him. (Numbers 20:20,21 NKJV).

[146] And command the people, saying, "You are about to pass through the territory of your brethren, the descendants of Esau, who live in Seir; and they will be afraid of you. Therefore watch yourselves carefully". (Deuteronomy 2:4 NKJV).

as the Lord's choice location to gather the remnant of Israel during the second Exodus. I believe this is the place in the wilderness referred to in Revelation 12 where the woman will find refuge away from the dragon for three and a half years. Edom is already prophesied as a place that will escape the Anti-Christ[147].

Those fleeing from Jerusalem on the Day of the Lord, will be gathered together with those who had gone before at the start of the great tribulation in Bozrah, as the sheepfold of the Lord. The nations that will seek Israel's demise and surround Jerusalem, will not succeed to complete her annihilation. What do we think those nations will do when they see the flight of those in Jerusalem join those already assembled in the wilderness? Having just witnessed the very return of the Lord Jesus Christ, will they now finally repent, and seek mercy at His feet? I don't think so! Did Pharaoh relent on his campaign against Israel, even after the waters of the Red Sea had been piled high on both sides to form a passage of escape right through the middle? Did Pharaoh then surmise he was no match for the wrath of God? No. Instead, blinded by his pride, his hardened heart and his hatred for God and His people, Pharaoh pursued the escaping Hebrew nation with his mighty chariots and horsemen right down through the middle of the parted Red Sea.

> *The very place of God's deliverance becomes the place of destruction for those who oppose the Deliverer.*

In the same way, neither will those nations who have set themselves against Israel relent in their pursuit of her, and so the demise and fall of the nations will begin in the wilderness of the peoples. This war

---

[147] He shall also enter the Glorious Land, and many countries shall be overthrown; but these shall escape from his hand: Edom, Moab, and the prominent people of Ammon. (Daniel 11:41 NKJV).

will reach its climax during the Armageddon campaign, but it begins here in Edom. Here's what Isaiah writes:

Who is this who comes from Edom, in crimsoned garments from Bozrah, he who is splendid in his apparel, marching in the greatness of his strength? "It is I, speaking in righteousness, mighty to save." 2 Why is your apparel red, and your garments like his who treads in the winepress? 3 "I have trodden the winepress alone, and from the peoples no one was with me; I trod them in my anger and trampled them in my wrath; their lifeblood spattered on my garments, and stained all my apparel. 4 For the day of vengeance was in my heart, and my year of redemption had come. 5 I looked, but there was no one to help; I was appalled, but there was no one to uphold; so my own arm brought me salvation, and my wrath upheld me. 6 I trampled down the peoples in my anger; I made them drunk in my wrath, and I poured out their lifeblood on the earth."
(Isaiah 63:1-6 ESV).

This intriguing passage in Isaiah 63, not only specifically mentions Bozrah as the place of great bloodshed, but also it reveals this day of carnage is the day of wrath, and of treading the winepress. It is described as the day of vengeance and the year of redemption[148]. Can you see the confluence here between all these passages? With these details we can accurately place this passage in Isaiah 63 during the time of the Lord upon the earth when He comes in the days of wrath which begin on the day of the Lord. Which begins the Second Exodus.

---

[148] Isaiah 63:4.

QB53 The Second Exodus (Part 7)

Hi everybody and welcome back for part seven in this series *The Second Exodus*. If you've just joined us, and not watched parts one to six, then it's a good idea to watch those as well because each episode builds upon the former to develop this teaching line upon line, precept upon precept. So where are we currently at in our timeline? Jesus has returned to earth as the Son of Man just as Matthew 24 teaches. At this time the Bride who is ready and waiting will be caught up to meet the Lord in the air and will be presented to the Father in Heaven, but this is not yet time for the wedding of the Lamb, for Israel is not fully saved, and therefore the wife has not yet made herself ready. First, Israel and the Lord have a date in the wilderness prophesied thousands of years earlier. Remember a key point in our studies is that when Jesus returns as the King of Kings and Lord of Lords in Revelation 19, He does so with His Bride, which means Israel has been saved prior to this moment and therefore necessitates an earlier period of time in which the Lord will come as the Son of Man to deliver Israel, gather her to Himself and enable her to be the wife who has made herself ready. This period of time is what I mean when I refer to *The Second Exodus*. Jesus will come for Israel right at the end of 1260 days immediately after the tribulation of those days. At that time Jerusalem will be surrounded by the nations of the world and in great peril. But the Lord will come and provide a means of escape by standing on the Mount of Olives which will be split into two to form a mountain pass, through which the survivors of the siege will flee. They will flee into the wilderness and will join those who have already sojourned there for the last three and a half years. This place Ezekiel calls the wilderness of the nations or peoples, and I believe a strong contender for its location will be Bozrah, the ancient capital of the Kingdom of Edom which is twenty miles southeast of the Dead Sea in the land of the nation Jordan.

This will be a place of great bloodshed and vengeance against the nations. Isaiah 63 specifically mentions Bozrah as where this will take place, as does Isaiah 34:1-8. Here's verses 4-6 NKJV:

4 All the host of heaven shall be dissolved, And the heavens shall be rolled up like a scroll; All their host shall fall down As the leaf falls from the vine, And as fruit falling from a fig tree. 5 For My sword shall be bathed in heaven; Indeed it shall come down on Edom, And on the people of My curse, for judgment. 6 The sword of the LORD is filled with blood, It is made overflowing with fatness, With the blood of lambs and goats, With the fat of the kidneys of rams. For the LORD has a sacrifice in Bozrah, And a great slaughter in the land of Edom.

Even though there are similarities between this great slaughter described in Isaiah chapters 34 and 63, and what is commonly known as the battle of Armageddon in Revelation 19, I do not believe them to be the same. Yes, on both occasions Jesus is described as wearing blood-stained garments (Isaiah 63:1,2[149] and

---

[149] Who is this who comes from Edom, With dyed garments from Bozrah, This One who is glorious in His apparel, Traveling in the greatness of His strength?--"I who speak in righteousness, mighty to save." Why is Your apparel red, And Your garments like one who treads in the winepress? (Isaiah 63:1,2 NKJV).

Revelation 19:13[150]), and on both occasions, there is mention of a sword. Isaiah 34:6 refers to *'the sword of the Lord filled with blood'*, and Revelation 19:15 as *'a sharp sword coming out of His mouth with which to strike down the nations'*, but there are differences also.

Firstly, the location of the slaughter Isaiah prophesied is in Bozrah, but there is another location of great slaughter that Joel speaks of as the valley of Jehoshaphat[151] or the valley of decision, which connects east Jerusalem to the Mount of Olives. Revelation also mentions a great slaughter outside the city in Revelation 14:19,20:

So the angel swung his sickle across the earth and gathered the grape harvest of the earth and threw it into the great winepress of the wrath of God. And the winepress was trodden outside the city, and blood flowed from the winepress, as high as a horse's bridle, for 1,600 stadia. [ESV]

So, these two slaughters happen at different locations, one in Bozrah, Edom, and the other just outside Jerusalem. But I believe there is another reason why these battles are not the same. That's because these two battles happen at different times. Am I saying there will be a battle before Armageddon? Absolutely! Although the battle seems rather one-sided and more of a slaughter. One happens at the beginning of God's wrath and the other at the end. There is also a shift in the focus of hostilities during this period. At first, and

---

[150] He was clothed with a robe dipped in blood, and His name is called The Word of God. (Revelation 19:13 NKJV).

[151] I will also gather all nations, and bring them down to the Valley of Jehoshaphat; And I will enter into judgment with them there On account of My people, My heritage Israel, Whom they have scattered among the nations; They have also divided up My land. .....Let the nations be wakened, and come up to the Valley of Jehoshaphat; For there I will sit to judge all the surrounding nations. (Joel 3:2,12 NKJV).

before the Lord returns, the nations will come against Israel and Jerusalem, this is where we place Zechariah 14 when Jerusalem is under siege. But destroying Israel and especially Jerusalem will prove to be impossible because the Lord will come amongst His people to fight for them. Consequently, the focus of hostilities will shift away from Jerusalem and towards the Lord because the Lamb is now upon the earth. Revelation 17:12-14 reads:

The ten horns which you saw are ten kings who have received no kingdom as yet, but they receive authority for one hour as kings with the beast. These are of one mind, and they will give their power and authority to the beast. These will make war with the Lamb, and the Lamb will conquer them, because he is Lord of lords and King of kings, and those with him are called and chosen and faithful. [NKJV]

This is a reference to the Battle of Armageddon which concludes the wrath of God. It is demonically induced[152] after the sixth bowl of wrath is poured out on the river Euphrates[153] and so comes right at the end of this period of wrath: the thirty days it will take between

---

[152] This demonic seduction is an important point because it gives a reason why those kings and peoples who initially try to flee from the wrath of God and the Lamb by hiding in the caves and amongst the rocks Revelation 6:15-17 are later found gathering for battle against the Lord.
[153] Then the sixth angel poured out his bowl on the great river Euphrates, and its water was dried up, so that the way of the kings from the east might be prepared. And I saw three unclean spirits like frogs coming out of the mouth of the dragon, out of the mouth of the beast, and out of the mouth of the false prophet. For they are spirits of demons, performing signs, which go out to the kings of the earth and of the whole world, to gather them to the battle of that great day of God Almighty. "Behold, I am coming as a thief. Blessed is he who watches, and keeps his garments, lest he walk naked and they see his shame." - And they gathered them together to the place called in Hebrew, Armageddon. (Revelation 16:12-16 NKJV).

the Beast losing his authority[154] to the end of the abomination of desolation[155]. This is when Jesus will return once more[156], and as Revelation 17:14 records, *'the Lamb will conquer His enemies because He is Lord or Lords and King of Kings'*, notice here also in this verse Jesus is accompanied by His Bride, the called, chosen and faithful.

But what of the earlier bloodshed in Edom? Why should there be, as Isaiah writes, *'a sacrifice in Bozrah, a great slaughter in the Land of Edom?'* I believe the nations who come against Israel and surround Jerusalem, after witnessing an almighty deliverance when the Lord returns with His holy ones, will not relent on their intent to see her downfall and will try again to destroy her, this time they will gather at Bozrah, to surround her once more. Is this what Micah foretold would happen? Let's read Micah 2:12,13 The Septuagint puts it like this:

Jacob shall be completely gathered with all his people: I will surely receive the remnant of Israel; I will cause them to return together, as sheep in trouble, as a flock in the midst of their fold: they shall rush forth from among men through the breach made before them: they have broken through, and passed the gate, and gone out by it: and their king has gone out before them, and the Lord shall lead them.

---

[154] And he was given a mouth speaking great things and blasphemies, and he was given authority to continue for forty-two months. (Revelation 13:5 NKJV).

[155] And from the time that the daily sacrifice is taken away, and the abomination of desolation is set up, there shall be one thousand two hundred and ninety days. (Daniel 12:11 NKJV).

[156] As we shall see later in Quick Bites 56-60 the Lord and redeemed Israel shall enter into Heaven for the Wedding of the Lamb at some point during this time of wrath upon the earth.

The Lord is the breaker, the Good Shepherd who will open up the breach, and pass on ahead of His people who will rush forth from among men. They will pass through the gate and shall leave the sheepfold, the enclosure of Bozrah. Into which they had been gathered as a flock in the midst of their fold. The return to Zion has begun!

Did you know that some claim this story is depicted in the stars and constellations of the night sky? It truly is a magnificent tale. For in the northern sky there is a constellation known as Draco, a serpentine dragon, which circles menacingly around another constellation which today is known as the Little Dipper, but in Ancient times was called the Lesser Sheepfold. I encourage you to find a star map that shows these two constellations, and you will see one star leading the others out of the Lesser Sheepfold which are all heading out of the enclosing threatening Draco. What's even more fascinating is that this lead star, is the North Star, also known as Polaris, because it is the one around which all the others move. Well, I'll leave you to research further, but thought it an interesting anecdote worthy of mention.

QB54 The Second Exodus (Part 8)

In this series, we have covered a lot of ground and some really difficult prophetic passages. I've chosen just a selection of verses available to piece together enough of a picture to help us understand a period of time I have called *'the Second Exodus'*, which commences upon the Day of the Lord (described in Matthew 24, when Jesus returns as the Son of Man), to the wedding of the Lamb which happens before His ultimate Return in Revelation 19 (as the King of Kings and Lord of Lords). This period of time, which as I shared in Quick Bites 45-46 will be a total of thirty days. There will be many things taking place during this time of wrath, but our focus has been upon Israel and how she is to be prepared for her wedding day. For her atonement there will be just ten days, which are known as the Days of Awe. These join the Feast of Trumpets, when Jesus returns, to the Day of Atonement, also known as Yom Kippur.

I believe there is good Biblical support for this viewpoint, and whilst I'm not stating these things as absolute, I am saying I believe them to be the best possible fit when considering the entirety of Biblical Prophecy. You see it is not good enough to focus on one area of eschatology, pull some scriptures together which support each other, and promote a subsection of the future when it does not stack up to other Biblical texts which contradict or oppose that view. Does it mean the Bible contradicts itself, absolutely not! It means there's a problem with the interpretation or presupposition we brought into the process. That's the challenge for the student of prophecy: how do you fit all the pieces together harmoniously? Well as you may have heard me say before, we need a blueprint, an end-time picture of what the Lord sees and desires, because that blueprint is the underlying influence upon all prophecy. I believe the Bride is that blueprint. When we see the Bride and understand who she is and how she will prepare, it is the key to unlock the unfolding of future events.

The Wife must make herself ready, and that means both Jew and Gentile. We can't side-line Israel's gathering, redemption, and wedding into a Millennial event, as though it were inconsequential and supplemental to the main story which belongs to the church. No, it doesn't belong to the church, the story belongs to the Elect, there's a subtle but important difference. One includes Israel, the other does not. The Lord will not tear the branch from the Olive tree, but He will cultivate them together as One, the One New Man, the Bride.[157]

---

[157] For I speak to you Gentiles; inasmuch as I am an apostle to the Gentiles, I magnify my ministry, if by any means I may provoke to jealousy those who are my flesh and save some of them. For if their being cast away is the reconciling of the world, what will their acceptance be but life from the dead? For if the firstfruit is holy, the lump is also holy; and if the root is holy, so are the branches. And if some of the branches were broken off, and you, being a wild olive tree, were grafted in among them, and with them became a partaker of the root and fatness of the olive tree, do not boast against the branches. But if you do boast, remember that you do not support the root, but the root supports you. You will say then, "Branches were broken off that I might be grafted in." Well said. Because of unbelief they were broken off, and you stand by faith. Do not be haughty, but fear. For if God did not spare the natural branches, He may not spare you either. (Romans 11:13-21 NKJV)

Matthew 24 speaks of the gathering of the Elect, thank God that it does. The pre-trib believer will say *'yes this is Israel'* and the post-trib advocate will say, *'no, the Lord is speaking to His church'.* Jesus could have easily mentioned either Israel or the Church as the intended crowd to be gathered, but He uses neither and says it will be His Elect who are gathered. That's because to mention either Israel or the Church as those gathered, would automatically exclude the other. The church will be gathered, but so will Israel.

On the Day of the Lord, Jesus will return as the Son of Man to gather His Elect, to gather His Bride. Those ready and waiting will be caught up together into the air at the first resurrection, but for unsaved Israel, the Son of Man's role as Saviour and Redeemer is not yet finished. The remnant of Israel, wherever they may be, will be gathered not up into the air, but to a location upon the earth. This gathering will not be at first to Israel but to a place Ezekiel calls the *'wilderness of the peoples'.* Listen again to Ezekiel:

And I will bring you out from the people, and will gather you out of the nations where you are scattered, with a mighty hand, and with a stretched out arm, and with fury poured out. And I will bring you into the wilderness of the people, and there will I plead [The word 'plead' also means to judge, govern, vindicate or punish] with you face to face. (Ezekiel 20:34,35). *[brackets mine]*

The point I want to make here is that it is a singular location not a dispersion but a convening, a gathering. The Lord said I will bring you out of and bring you into. I will bring you out from the people and gather you out of the nations where you are scattered, and I will bring you into, into the wilderness, into the wilderness of the people, which is also called the wilderness of the nations.

It is here He will meet with them face to face. This location does not describe the current dispersion of the Jews, it is the place they will be brought into not out from. Now in this wilderness location there will be a sifting of the sheepfold of Israel.

37 I will make you pass under the rod, and I will bring you into the bond of the covenant; 38 I will purge the rebels from among you, and those who transgress against Me; I will bring them out of the country where they dwell, but they shall not enter the land of Israel. Then you will know that I am the LORD. (Ezekiel 20:37-38 NKJV).

The Lord said they will all be brought out of the countries where they dwell and were previously scattered and they will be brought into the wilderness of the nations, where there will be a purging, and the rebels will be sifted out[158]. Ezekiel 34:17 says the Lord will judge His flock, judging between one sheep and another. They will pass under the rod. Leviticus 27:32[159] describes this act of passing under the rod as a way to select a tenth of all animals from the herd or flock and dedicate them to the Lord as holy. In this sense, not all Israel

---

[158] This concept of purging by denying entry into the promised land is not unfamiliar. We are well informed out of all those who fled Egypt it was only Joshua and Caleb who found that blessed rest. We see this principle variously in scripture such as found in Ezekiel 13:9[NET] which reads "My hand will be against the prophets who see delusion and announce lying omens. They will not be included in the council of my people, nor be written in the registry of the house of Israel, nor enter the land of Israel. Then you will know that I am the Sovereign LORD."

[159] And concerning the tithe of the herd or the flock, of whatever passes under the rod, the tenth one shall be holy to the LORD. (Leviticus 27:32 NKJV).

will be saved[160]. Not all Israel will enter their homeland. Just as in the first Exodus not all those who left Egypt returned to Canaan, but they perished in the wilderness, so also not all those who are gathered into the wilderness will return to Zion. Judgement will begin first with the Jews and then with the Greek[161]. Indeed, remember this time of judgement and sifting will be during those ten days of awe. It will be one final opportunity for those whose names are not written in the Book of Life to repent before the ultimate prophetic fulfilment of Yom Kippur, the Day of Atonement. Then, as Ezekiel writes, those chosen shall be brought into the bond of the covenant. What covenant do we suppose this may be? Well let's look at another favourite passage of mine found in Hosea:

14 "Therefore, behold, I will allure her, I will bring her into the wilderness, And speak comfort to her. 15 I will give her her vineyards from there, And the Valley of Achor as a door of hope; She shall sing there, As in the days of her youth, As

---

[160] The concept of 'all Israel will be saved' should not be seen numerically but inclusively. That is 'all' does not mean every individual Israelite but is an expression of breadth. All the tribes and those who have been grafted in.

For if you were cut out of the olive tree which is wild by nature, and were grafted contrary to nature into a cultivated olive tree, how much more will these, who are natural branches, be grafted into their own olive tree? For I do not desire, brethren, that you should be ignorant of this mystery, lest you should be wise in your own opinion, that blindness in part has happened to Israel until the fullness of the Gentiles has come in. And so all Israel will be saved, as it is written: 'The Deliverer will come out of Zion, And He will turn away ungodliness from Jacob' (Romans 11:24-26 NKJV).

[161] but to those who are self-seeking and do not obey the truth, but obey unrighteousness--indignation and wrath, tribulation and anguish, on every soul of man who does evil, of the Jew first and also of the Greek; but glory, honour, and peace to everyone who works what is good, to the Jew first and also of the Greek. (Romans 2:8-10 NKJV).

in the day when she came up from the land of Egypt. 16 And it shall be, in that day," Says the LORD, "That you will call Me 'My Husband,' And no longer call Me 'My Master,' 17 For I will take from her mouth the names of the Baals, And they shall be remembered by their name no more. 18 In that day I will make a covenant for them With the beasts of the field, With the birds of the air, And with the creeping things of the ground. Bow and sword of battle I will shatter from the earth, To make them lie down safely. 19 I will betroth you to Me forever; Yes, I will betroth you to Me In righteousness and justice, In lovingkindness and mercy; 20 I will betroth you to Me in faithfulness, And you shall know the LORD. 21 It shall come to pass in that day That I will answer," says the LORD; "I will answer the heavens, And they shall answer the earth. 22 The earth shall answer With grain, with new wine, And with oil; They shall answer Jezreel. 23 Then I will sow her for Myself in the earth, And I will have mercy on her who had not obtained mercy; Then I will say to those who were not My people, 'You are My people!' And they shall say, 'You are my God!' " (Hosea 2:14-23 NKJV).

Wow, what an amazing prophecy that fits so beautifully into our Bridal perspective on the end times. Through this entire series on the Second Exodus the underlying question has been: how does the wife make herself ready? Because when Jesus comes as the Son of Man in Matthew 24, the wife will not yet be ready because Israel will not yet be fully saved, and there can be no wedding without her. Those already in the New Covenant will be raptured upon the Lord's coming, but what of unsaved Israel? For a brief period of time the Bride will be in Heaven and upon the Earth. This has been the subject of this series, how Israel is brought back into the marriage covenant, so the wife can complete her preparations. For that to happen she is led into the wilderness to be romanced by the Lord. Ezekiel has told us those who pass under the rod will come into the covenant, and Hosea 2 is a beautiful prophecy which describes this betrothal and renewal of their first love.

> *There in the wilderness Israel will sing, just as she did when she came up before from the land of Egypt. It is there Israel will call the Lord her husband, and there the Lord will betroth her to Himself forever.*

I'm just speechless, what beauty, what majesty, what glory there is contained in this most wonderful romance between the Lord and His Bride. Thank God, He has not forsaken Israel. Not in the least! Our God is faithful to His promise and we all, whether Jew or Gentile, shall be made one. We shall be ready and then united with our Bridegroom Jesus Christ forever. This is the glory that awaits us, the hope of our faith, the certainty of our calling, and the resolute cry of our hearts, in which we cry, *"Maranatha, Even so, Come Lord Jesus Come!"*

QB55 The Second Exodus (Part 9)

The Bride will be prepared in the wilderness. It is here that we can make our final wedding preparations. The wilderness is not a place of suffering or misery or self-pity, but it is the place of romance. It is the place where we are separated out from the crowds into solitude so we can be alone with Him. It is the place of intimacy. In a very real sense, the Lord is leading His Bride into the wilderness today, into a place where the stars shine more brightly and where the waters from the ravine are pure.

> *O that we might find the well in the desert and know its Source who is Christ. O that we may cherish this most holy and secret place. The Bride loves the desert. She sings in the desert; she turns the Valley of Baka into refreshing springs* [162]

But this wilderness is not only a metaphor, for the remnant of Israel it will be a very real and literal place.

14 "Therefore, behold, I will allure her, Will bring her into the wilderness, And speak comfort to her. 15 I will give her her vineyards from there, And the Valley of Achor as a door of hope; She shall sing there, As in the days of her youth, As in the day when she came up from the land of Egypt. 16 And it

---

[162] As they pass through the Valley of Baca, They make it a spring; The rain also covers it with pools. (Psalm 84:6 NKJV).

shall be, in that day," Says the LORD, "That you will call Me 'My Husband,' And no longer call Me 'My Master,'" (Hosea 2:14-16 NKJV).

Did you know the wilderness is the place of betrothal? This is how it was for Israel on the first Exodus when Moses led the nation into the wilderness and came to Mount Sinai. Hosea goes on to write in verse 19:

I will betroth you to Me forever. (Hosea 2:19 NKJV).

Once the Bride has been purified in the wilderness, she will return home on a highway of Holiness. Here's what Isaiah wrote about this coming great moment:

4 Say to those who are fearful-hearted, "Be strong, do not fear! Behold, your God will come with vengeance, With the recompense of God; He will come and save you." 5 Then the eyes of the blind shall be opened, And the ears of the deaf shall be unstopped. 6 Then the lame shall leap like a deer, And the tongue of the dumb sing. For waters shall burst forth in the wilderness, And streams in the desert. 7 The parched ground shall become a pool, And the thirsty land springs of water; In the habitation of jackals, where each lay, There shall be grass with reeds and rushes. 8 A highway shall be there, and a road, And it shall be called the Highway of Holiness. The unclean shall not pass over it, But it shall be for others. Whoever walks the road, although a fool, Shall not go astray. 9 No lion shall be there, Nor shall any ravenous beast go up on it; It shall not be found there. But the redeemed shall walk there, 10 And the ransomed of the LORD shall return, And come to Zion with singing, With everlasting joy on their heads. They shall obtain joy and

gladness, And sorrow and sighing shall flee away. (Isaiah 35:4-10 NKJV).

Hallelujah. Praise God. I believe this passage in Isaiah is another clear reference to the time of the Second Exodus as we have been learning, when the Lord will come to deliver His people by leading them out into the wilderness. Isaiah begins in this passage with a word of encouragement, saying to those who are afraid, he says, *'Be Strong and do not fear, because your God will come'* and when He comes, He will *'come with vengeance'*. This is a reference to the Day of the Lord when the wrath of the Lamb shall come. On that Day the Lord will come and He will save His people. As we have already seen previously, this will be when Jerusalem is surrounded by the nations of the world. Isaiah foresees a time when *'the eyes of the blind shall be opened, And the ears of the deaf shall be unstopped,'* but then we are transported away from Jerusalem into the wilderness where Isaiah describes how *'waters shall burst forth in the wilderness, And streams in the desert'*, where the *'parched ground shall become a pool'*. Isaiah has taken us to see this wilderness location where the redeemed shall be gathered, and he sees in this wilderness a highway, which shall be called *'the Highway of Holiness'*. It will be a safe passage upon which *'the redeemed shall walk'* and *'the ransomed of the Lord shall return'*. To where will they return? It will be to *'Zion with singing'* and *'everlasting joy shall be upon their heads'*. Gladness and joy shall be theirs, and *'sorrow and mourning shall flee away'*.

They shall come and sing aloud on the height of Zion, and they shall be radiant over the goodness of the LORD, over the grain, the wine, and the oil, and over the young of the flock and the herd; their life shall be like a watered garden, and they shall languish no more. 13 Then shall the young women rejoice in the dance, and the young men and the old shall be merry. I will turn their mourning into joy; I will comfort them, and give them gladness for sorrow. (Jeremiah 31:12,13 ESV).

After all of Jerusalem's suffering, Jacob's trouble, the great tribulation and the persecution of the nations, God shall redeem His people and they shall sing and rejoice and dance once more in the Bridegroom Bride relationship. For God will restore them into the covenant of a marriage relationship He has with His people. This completes the Second Exodus of Israel's escape from her enemies surrounding Jerusalem, into the wilderness to be prepared as the wife who has made herself ready. Remember all this time, the Bride has been both in Heaven and upon the Earth. The objective has always been to bring the two together, to complete the Bride and to prepare her for her wedding day. This has always necessitated the salvation of Israel. Unless you believe the gentile church is raptured prematurely and married whilst Israel is still in great tribulation upon the earth, then there must be a time to bring convergence and unification of the two into One New Man, because there is only one bride. Now we have journeyed with Israel through her deliverance, redemption, preparation and return to Zion with singing, I will finish this series with one remaining question: If the Wedding of the Lamb takes place in Heaven, how do those returning back to Israel, back to Zion, enter into Heaven for the wedding? Since the rapture or the gathering up into the clouds when the Lord comes as the Son of Man has already happened, does that mean there is another rapture now for returning Israel? Or is there some other way in which Israel shall be admitted? I can't wait to share the answer with you, but that will be where we continue next time as I begin a new series and take a look at Revelation 14 and the mysterious 144,000. May the Lord bless you richly.

QB56 The 144,000 (Part 1)

W ell, what a journey we have been on through this series of Quick Bites, exploring many difficult and sometimes controversial topics relating to the end-times, and one of the key principles I have adopted through this volume of teaching, has been the necessity to approach scripture, and in particular eschatology from a Bridal perspective. When we don't look at prophecy through the Bridal lens, we are prone to come up with many different views and opinions on such matters of the future, which at times has only served to fragment and harm the church, which is the complete opposite of why the scriptures and prophecy have been given in the first place, which is to be our guide to life and our blueprint for how the Bride should get ready. How then can prophecy lead to division? When prophetic interpretation leads to division and strife, we seriously have to question the very doctrinal foundation upon which we stand.

But when we are prepared to lay down previously held positions of eschatological thought, and allow our fingers to be prised away from what we hold onto so dearly (because in them we have found a measure of understanding), then we are ready to look again at the Biblical narrative without the presuppositions we once held, and we are able to revisit the Word of God, without the temptation to fit scripture into our former beliefs as though looking for confirmation of an old mindset, rather than a willingness to let those beliefs be scrutinised and revised.

> *If the Bride is to truly prepare. then she must learn this lesson well. She must embrace the Bridal paradigm and allow her vision and Biblical compass to be recalibrated accordingly.*

But there is more at stake here than just her preparation, for preparation does not take place in a vacuum devoid of who she is and what she has been called to. Her preparation is not a passive act of waiting for her rapture to escape the impending night of a world increasingly destined for judgment, but is a radical pro-activity, clothed in humility and holiness, yes, but she is a warrior, a prophetess, and mightily empowered to do great exploits. She is no cowering violet hiding in the shadows. Is that a Bride worthy of betrothal to the King of Kings and Lord of Lords? I don't think so! She will reach a place in her devotion that is uncompromising, and she will not bow the knee to any idol. There will be something wild, something untamed about her, a rare beauty of an untethered soul, she will show a ferocity for holiness, and yet a gentleness like a lamb. Her heart will overflow with such love, and her words will be filled with wisdom and great insight. Throughout this process, the Bride will resemble her Bridegroom with increasing glory.

This is our passion, our vision, and our mandate: to prepare the Bride to become all that she was created to be, and to fulfil all that she has been mandated to do. It requires a solid Biblical exegesis, upon which she is not left disorientated, confused or unaware of who she is or what lies ahead, but rather a firm scriptural foundation upon which she can depend as though her very life depended upon it, because that's exactly the point, it does depend on it!

So, this has been my hope and prayer, that in writing this volume of Quick Bites, it has been as though I were writing '*The Gospel according to the Bride*. To give her a voice, so she might help us to understand what she knows, and to see what has been revealed to her. By adopting the Bridal paradigm, we are given a glimpse into her world, without which we would simply be none the wiser, but as the writer of Hebrews instructs:

Therefore, let us move beyond the elementary teachings about Christ and be taken forward to maturity (perfection and spiritual completeness) (Hebrews 6:1a NIV brackets mine).

With this in mind, I will complete this first volume of *'The Gospel According to the Bride'*, as promised, with a new series on the 144,000. If you remember, in our previous study *'The Second Exodus'*, it was always necessary for Jesus to return as the Son of Man, to complete the work of salvation, not only for those who eagerly await His appearing, but also for the Nation of Israel, upon which so much depends. For ultimately, there can be no Bride, and no wedding without her, for as the apostle Paul writes:

Theirs is the adoption as sons; theirs the divine glory and the covenants; theirs the giving of the law, the temple worship, and the promises. (Romans 9:4 BSB).

Where we ended *'The Second Exodus'* series was upon the return of saved Israel, who had been gathered into the *'wilderness of the nations'*, but now were returning on the *'Highway of Holiness'*[163], back to Mount Zion with great rejoicing, singing and dancing [164]. The New

---

[163] A highway shall be there, and a road, And it shall be called the Highway of Holiness. The unclean shall not pass over it, But it shall be for others. Whoever walks the road, although a fool, Shall not go astray. (Isaiah 35:8 NKJV).
[164] And the ransomed of the LORD shall return, And come to Zion with singing, With everlasting joy on their heads. They shall obtain joy and gladness, And sorrow and sighing shall flee away. (Isaiah 35:10 NKJV).

Covenant with Israel has been ratified, the Day of Atonement fulfilled, and the closing question we asked was this: If the Wedding of the Lamb takes place in Heaven, how do those returning back to Israel, back to Zion, enter into Heaven for the wedding? Since the rapture or the gathering up into the clouds when the Lord comes as the Son of Man has already happened, does that mean there is another rapture now for returning Israel? Or is there some other way in which Israel shall be admitted? It's a really good question, and it deserves a really good answer, which I'm excited to get to. but before we go deeper into this study, I'll finish today with the two passages which refer specifically to the 144,000 as the springboard for next time:

After these things I saw four angels standing at the four corners of the earth, holding the four winds of the earth, that the wind should not blow on the earth, on the sea, or on any tree. 2. Then I saw another angel ascending from the east, having the seal of the living God. And he cried with a loud voice to the four angels to whom it was granted to harm the earth and the sea, 3. saying, "Do not harm the earth, the sea, or the trees till we have sealed the servants of our God on their foreheads." 4. And I heard the number of those who were sealed. One hundred and forty-four thousand of all the tribes of the children of Israel were sealed: (Revelation 7:1-4 NKJV).

John then accounts for twelve thousand sealed from each of the tribes of Israel. We then come across these 144,000 again in Revelation 14:1-5:

Then I looked, and behold, a Lamb standing on Mount Zion, and with Him one hundred and forty-four thousand, having His Father's name written on their foreheads. 2. And I heard a voice from heaven, like the voice of many waters, and like the voice of loud thunder. And I heard the sound of harpists playing their harps. 3. They sang as it were a new song before the throne, before the four living creatures, and the elders; and no one could learn that song except the hundred and forty-four thousand who were redeemed from the earth. 4. These are the ones who were not defiled with women, for they are virgins. These are the ones who follow the Lamb wherever He goes. These were redeemed from among men, being firstfruits to God and to the Lamb. 5. And in their mouth was found no deceit, for they are without fault before the throne of God. [NKJV]

Fascinating, isn't it? Well, this is where we'll pick up next time.

QB57 The 144,000 (Part 2)

Today I will lay out some principles of good biblical exegesis that we will need if we are to comprehend and interpret the mystery of the 144,000. These principles will provide guidelines for us to follow and a filter with which we can purify and shape our understanding. There are five principles I'm going to share, which are actually questions to ask when approaching this or any Biblical passage. These principles, or questions, will help enormously to lay a reliable framework in which to make our conclusions. Without them, as we shall see, it would be easy to derail from a sound interpretation. So let's get started.

- The first principle (or question) is this: What does the scripture actually say in the plain sense meaning of the text?

- The second principle (or question) follows this by asking the opposite, which is: What doesn't the passage say?

- Then third, we ask: Are there any other scriptures which shed further light and understanding on the text?

- Our fourth principle asks: What is the context into which the Bible verses are placed?

- And last. but not least, our fifth principle asks: Should we apply a literal or metaphorical meaning to the text?

Okay, let's now apply these principles to the passages we find in Revelation 7:1-8 and Revelation 14:1-5 which describe a group of people known as the 144,000. After reading the verses in Revelation 7 let's apply our first principle and ask: what does this passage actually say in its plain sense meaning? Well at first glance this would seem easily answered because John hears quite clearly; these 144,000 are numbered as twelve thousand from each of the twelve tribes of Israel. Thus, if we went no further in our analysis, we could come to no other opinion than these are all Israelites. To take any other view would require a solid biblical reason in which to deviate. Now, whether such justification exists or not, I shall come to later in this series, but for now let's anchor this point in place: that without further scrutiny these 144,000 are as simply stated, they are all Israelites.

Okay, now for our second principle or question: What doesn't this passage say? Well for a start, it doesn't say they are the church. The angel speaking with John goes into great detail, verse after verse, to list all the tribes in turn with twelve thousand from each, as though to underline and emphasise their identity in no uncertain terms. To simply disregard this detailed account and replace Israel for the church would be a gross deviation away from the plain sense meaning of the text and whether in this passage, or indeed any biblical passage, we must tread very carefully when tempted to deviate away from the simplest interpretation. I'm not saying we can't explore alternate meaning; indeed, we should always explore beyond that which is presented to us at face value, but we must have very good reasons to do so.

Now, what else doesn't this passage say about these 144,000? Nowhere in Revelation 7:1-8 or its sister passage in Revelation 14:1-5 is there any mention or even a hint of these people being evangelists! This is a key point, and is the popular pre-tribulation view, which in my opinion arises from bad exegesis and is a great example of eisegesis. To clarify what I mean, let me explain the difference between exegesis and eisegesis. Exegesis is the process of taking the original intended meaning out of scripture, whereas eisegesis is the process of reading into the scripture something that isn't there, normally because of our own preconceptions and beliefs. We can all do this, especially when we prioritise existing beliefs over scriptural texts. In other words, eisegesis can happen when we read a text with a presumption or preferred viewpoint and seek to apply that opinion or belief into the text. For example, the reason many see the 144,000 as evangelists is because of the second group of people listed in Revelation 7:9-17 – the great multitude which no one could number from every tribe and nation, people and tongue who come out of the great tribulation. Now since the pre-tribulation view presupposes the saved are raptured before the great tribulation, this great multitude must be saved after the rapture which would necessitate an army of evangelists still present upon the earth during this time, hence the theory which proposes the only candidates for this army are the 144,000. However, I must point out this would immediately raise other problems. Since any messianic Jew would be raptured, who would lead the unsaved tribes of Israel to the Lord? In my humble opinion, the view of the 144,000 as evangelists is a textbook clear example of eisegesis since there is no suggestion, zero indication within the text that this is the case.

In fact, nowhere in the Revelation 7 passage is there any other description of this crowd except their number and their descendancy. For further description we must look at Revelation 14:1-5 which does give more detail on their actions and identity, which brings us to our third principle: Are there any other passages which shed further light? The answer is of course yes, Revelation 14:1-5 does shed further light and describes this number as being redeemed, as those who follow the Lamb. The Lamb of course, is a picture of Jesus Christ as the Saviour. This answers our fourth principle about context. The context here in Revelation 14 is about redemption, about salvation and purity. The Bible describes them as first fruits. Surely if they were in any way commissioned as evangelists here is an opportunity to say so. The truth is, it's not about the salvation of others, but their own, about their redemption, and about them following the Lamb wherever He goes. Unlike Jesus first coming, when He sent out the apostles to evangelise, here Jesus is not sending, but He's gathering and He's leading. He's on the move and the 144,000 are following the Lamb wherever He goes, they aren't being sent out, but they have followed the Lamb to Mount Zion. Now where have we heard that before?

If you followed my teaching on *'the Second Exodus'*, (and if not, then I encourage you to do so) you may remember how the tribes of Israel will be gathered into the wilderness of the peoples (Ezekiel 20:33-38), where they will be brought into the bond of the covenant, into the wedding covenant. There they will be purged and as Isaiah 51:11 reads:

therefore the redeemed of the Lord shall return and come with signing unto Zion and everlasting joy shall be upon their head; they shall obtain gladness and joy; and sorrow and mourning shall flee away. [KJV]

This is another great example of our third principle letting scripture interpret scripture. So, at this stage in our quest to identify the 144,000 it would seem unquestionable they are indeed Israelites. We have applied the first four principles, of what the passage says and what it doesn't say, what is the context and a brief look at other scripture to shed further light.

Their identity as from the twelve tribes of Israel has stood up to our examination, which leads us to our fifth and final principle which asks the question: Does this passage have a literal or symbolic meaning? If we take the literal approach, and there is good reason to do so, then our study is complete, we can close our notebooks and move on, having satisfied ourselves that these 144,000 are Israelites, they are not evangelists, but are those who have been redeemed in the wilderness and have now followed Jesus back to Mount Zion.

But is it really this simple? Because the literal approach does present some challenges, which you may not be aware of. For example, if we adopt the literal approach, then does that mean the Lamb is a literal lamb? Clearly not! But if we accept the Lamb as a metaphor for Jesus, then we have from the outset already treated this passage as partly symbolic. And once we open the door to symbolism, we suddenly increase the complexity of our challenge to understand the passage. Where do we draw the line between that which is a metaphor and that which is literal? If the Lamb is a metaphor, what else is a metaphor? For example, the Revelation 14 passage describes them as all male virgins, but in Jeremiah 31:12,13[165] we read how women are included among their number, suggesting this is another metaphor, and so you can see how we have quickly moved from being in a position to make our decision, and suddenly entered into a whole new dilemma. But what if there were some other clues to help us unravel this mystery? What if there were another perspective

---

[165] They shall come and sing aloud on the height of Zion, and they shall be radiant over the goodness of the LORD, over the grain, the wine, and the oil, and over the young of the flock and the herd; their life shall be like a watered garden, and they shall languish no more. Then shall the young women rejoice in the dance, and the young men and the old shall be merry. I will turn their mourning into joy; I will comfort them, and give them gladness for sorrow. (Jeremiah 31:12,13 ESV).

with which we could view this 144,000, a lens to see something we haven't seen before? I believe there is, and the answer has been right in front of us all this time.

QB58 The 144,000 (Part 3)

In our study so far of the 144,000, we have set out a framework of good biblical exegesis to provide a means by which we might make our conclusions over their identity. Now I'd like to make a disclaimer at this point, that in no way do I want to make the things I'm sharing with you an absolute or as '*the*' right interpretation. I don't want to come across that way but rather in all humility share with you some insights and scriptures from my own study and prayer as I have sought the Lord in the hope that these things may be of value to you. As we saw last time, taking the literal approach with Revelation 7:1-8 and its sister passage in Revelation 14:1-5 is not entirely possible, for there are several elements within these verses that are clearly not literal and has to be taken symbolically. Now it doesn't mean we dismiss the tribes of Israel and replace them with the church, or that their number isn't significant, indeed there is a reason we are given 144,000, which so clearly shouts at us from the pages of our Bibles, as though to draw our attention to this number.

The question I left us with last time, was whether there is a clue within these two passages in Revelation to provide a lens by which we might gaze deeper into understanding who these 144,000 are? The answer is of course yes, and the clue we are given is the actual number 144,000 itself. So today I want to go into some really interesting numerology, but before I do so, it's important to understand whilst Biblical numerology can be very helpful, it can also be wrongly used and come up with all kinds of misleading conclusions and permutations. That's because numbers in themselves can be put together in many different ways: by adding, subtracting, multiplying and dividing occurrences or patterns we find in the Word of God we can easily fall into error.

> *So here is a principle I like to adopt when considering biblical numerology: Any words or numbers we consider should only be used to support a principle that already exists in the Bible, in other words, numbers have a supporting role not a primary one.*

We are not looking to fit scripture around the numbers, but the numbers to confirm and highlight what the scripture is already saying.

With that said, I want to take you on a journey in which we will follow a numerical footprint. If you know where to look you will find this trail throughout the Old and New Testaments, but because of time, I will start at the end and work backwards from there. Since this volume of Quick Bites is called '*The Gospel According to the Bride*', it should come as no surprise then, that these are her footprints, this is her pathway, her journey that we see through scripture and her trail leads us right up to her glorious unveiling in Revelation 21[166]. But let's pick it up from verses 9-18 in which John is given some details of her formation.

Then one of the seven angels who had the seven bowls filled with the seven last plagues came to me and talked with me, saying, "Come, I will show you the bride, the Lamb's wife." 10

---

[166] If then you were raised with Christ, seek those things which are above, where Christ is, sitting at the right hand of God. Set your mind on things above, not on things on the earth. For you died, and your life is hidden with Christ in God. When Christ [who is] our life appears, then you also will appear with Him in glory. (Colossians 4:1-4 NKJV)

And he carried me away in the Spirit to a great and high mountain, and showed me the great city, the holy Jerusalem, descending out of heaven from God, 11 having the glory of God. Her light was like a most precious stone, like a jasper stone, clear as crystal. 12 Also she had a great and high wall with twelve gates, and twelve angels at the gates, and names written on them, which are the names of the twelve tribes of the children of Israel: 13 three gates on the east, three gates on the north, three gates on the south, and three gates on the west. 14 Now the wall of the city had twelve foundations, and on them were the names of the twelve apostles of the Lamb. 15 And he who talked with me had a gold reed to measure the city, its gates, and its wall. 16 The city is laid out as a square; its length is as great as its breadth. And he measured the city with the reed: twelve thousand furlongs. Its length, breadth, and height are equal. 17 Then he measured its wall: one hundred and forty-four cubits, according to the measure of a man, that is, of an angel. 18 The construction of its wall was of jasper; and the city was pure gold, like clear glass. [NKJV]

In verse sixteen we are told the height, length and breadth of the New Jerusalem, of the Bride, are all the same, that is 12,000 furlongs (or stadia[167]). To help simplify things, if we call 1,000 furlongs (or stadia) a Jerusalem Unit, then the volume or total size of the City would be 12x12x12 Jerusalem Units which is 1,728. Don't worry if you're wondering where I'm going with this, all will become clear

---

[167] A stadion (plural stadia) was an ancient Greece unit of length that the Greek historian Herodotus defined as 600 feet. If so, then 12,000 stadia is about 1,400 miles (or 2,200 kilometres). The length of a stadion is contested however because the measurement of a foot varied in different parts of ancient Greece.

soon enough. But for now, just remember the size of the New Jerusalem is 1,728 units.

There is a process known as gematria of assigning a numerical value to a word or phrase based upon its letters. In this way, the numerical value of Jerusalem is 864. Now this might not mean much at first until we realise that 864 is half of 1,728 the number of the New Jerusalem. Or let me put it like this, to arrive numerically at the size of the New Jerusalem, or the Bride, we need to add two Jerusalems together. And in Matthew 23:37 and Luke 13:34 this is exactly what we find. Here's what Matthew writes:

O Jerusalem, Jerusalem, the one who kills the prophets and stones those who are sent to her! How often I wanted to gather your children together, as a hen gathers her chicks under her wings, but you were not willing! [NKJV]

The value of O Jerusalem, Jerusalem is 1,728 which is the size of the New Jerusalem found in Revelation 21. Though not conclusive I do find that really interesting and wonder whether this verse of Jesus' longing to gather Jerusalem, is a prophetic picture of His longing to gather His Bride. But what does Jerusalem have to do with the 144,000? Well, did you know the word for Jerusalem is found 144 times in the New Testament? That's right, and you can check this out for yourselves with a Strong's Concordance using the references G2419, G2414 and G2415. Similarly, the numerical value of *The Election'* as in the chosen '*Eklektos*' of God is also 144. In Quick Bites 36 to 38, we saw how the Elect were the Bride, so all these numbers are wonderfully linked together, and at the root of them all is the number 144, which of course is the product of multiplying 12 by 12. One last point, before we pick up on this more next time, in Revelation 21:17 it reads:

Then he (that is the angel) measured its wall: one hundred and forty-four cubits, according to the measure of a man, that is, of an angel. [NKJV]

Here we are given the actual wall measurement, which is 144 cubits[168], confirming once more the significance of this number as Bridal, but there's a really important addendum which is easily missed, for tagged onto the end of this verse it says, *'that is, of an angel'*. In other words, when measuring the Bride, there is a calibration between the measurement of man, and the measurement of the angel. They are the same. That's because both heaven and earth are agreed on the dimensions of the Bride! Wow, what an amazing insight, but more than this, man cannot count the Bride unless he's using the measurement of the angel, otherwise he'll come up with a different number. To measure the Bride we need God's ruler, His measurement. We need our discernment and perspective to be calibrated accordingly to the measurement of the angel. Well, we'll pick up from here next time.

---

[168] Though the exact length of a cubit is disputed it is largely accepted as approximately eighteen inches. Ultimately in this context it doesn't matter, because the point I'm making is that both the angel and man use the same measurement.

QB59 The 144,000 (Part 4)

W e are coming to the end of our journey through scripture following the footsteps of the Bridegroom and the Bride. This has been their story and throughout all these Quick Bites we have heard *'The Gospel According to the Bride'*. Even though we have covered a lot of subjects in our studies, I feel we have only just scratched the surface of this most wonderful of all Biblical paradigms and realities. My prayer has always been that you will be encouraged and inspired to see just how much the Lord loves His Bride and will do everything necessary to ensure she is ready in time for their Wedding.

In the first two parts of this mini-series we began by taking the literal approach since this is the simplest and plainest interpretation of the 144,000. We read in Revelation 7:1-8 how John heard this number was comprised of 12,000 from each of the tribes of Israel. Hence this was our starting place: the 144,000 does represent Israel and we would require a very solid reason to deviate away from this interpretation. After all, if this number were not Israel, then why go to such great length to describe their number in this intricate detail? However, we cannot close our study and conclusions at this point, because in many ways, both the Revelation 7 and Revelation 14 passages do contain some metaphor and non-literal details; not least the Lamb in Revelation 14 is clearly symbolic and depicts the Lord Jesus Christ. But more than this, the picture of the Lamb illustrates the Lord as the atoning sacrifice which is consistent with the context of the Revelation passages, which as we saw in Revelation 14:3, describe the 144,000 as being redeemed from the earth. By taking only the literal approach the meaning of the text is partially obscured, and therefore we must be willing to consider the figurative also. But therein lies the problem: because as soon as we deviate away from the literal, we immediately open the door to subjectivity. The challenge we are faced with is how to incorporate both the literal and metaphorical interpretation without one cancelling out the other. Is there a way in which literal Israel remains represented by this number even though the number itself can be argued as representational? Is there a way in which this 144,000 represents Israel but not exclusively?

I shared last time in part three how to approach this passage metaphorically, and the clue or key is in the number itself. I suggested that 144 is the number of the Bride and is the agreed measurement for the Bride between man and the angel in Revelation 21:17[169].

> *Therefore, I further suggest that though the tribes of Israel are literal, their number speaks more of their Bridal identity than the size of their population. 144,000 is not arbitrary, not just a number without meaning, but it represents who they are and how the Lord sees them; He is attributing to the tribes of Israel their Bridal identity.*

If we can accept this point, then it follows all those numbered as the Bride are included in this number also. In other words, the 144,000 has a dual application! It represents those tribes of Israel who shall be redeemed when the Son of Man (the Lamb of God) comes for

---

[169] Then he measured its wall: one hundred and forty-four cubits, according to the measure of a man, that is, of an angel. (Revelation 21:17 NKJV).

them as we have studied previously in the Second Exodus series, but it also represents the entirety of the Bride both Jew and Gentile. I believe this position is consistent with other scriptures and emphatically places Israel at the heart of the Bridal paradigm, and any inclusion within the Bride is only possible by the covenant made between the Lord and her. This is what John saw in Revelation 21:12[170], the twelve gates having the names of the twelve tribes written upon them. Anyone who enters into the New Jerusalem will have done so through the gates of Israel.

Yet I should point out I do not refer to geopolitical Israel, nor the unregenerate Israel of the Old Testament. But when we consider all the wonderful promises God made with Israel through the Law and the Prophets, we must understand these are fulfilled through the work and person of Jesus Christ.

> *Yes, the promises and covenant were made to Israel, but their fulfilment is through the atoning work and person of Jesus Christ, who fulfilled the spring feasts on His first coming, and will fulfil the prophetic significance of the autumn feasts on His second.*

Even literal Israel cannot be numbered among the Bride without first accepting Jesus Christ for all that He is and all that He has accomplished for her.[171] That's why He's coming back for her, to bring her into the New Covenant, Zechariah 12:10 reads:

---

[170] Also she had a great and high wall with twelve gates, and twelve angels at the gates, and names written on them, which are the names of the twelve tribes of the children of Israel (Revelation 21:12 NKJV).

[171] Hence the walls (and therefore the gates) are upon the foundations inscribed with the names of the apostles of the Lamb. Note, these twelve

And I will pour on the house of David and on the inhabitants of Jerusalem the Spirit of grace and supplication; then they will look on Me whom they pierced. Yes, they will mourn for Him as one mourns for his only son, and grieve for Him as one grieves for a firstborn. [NKJV]

Now, finally as promised, I want to share my understanding of how those redeemed from Israel, who have been brought down into the wilderness of the peoples[172], sifted, redeemed, and now returned home to Mount Zion, will enter into Heaven for the wedding of the Lamb. Let me explain the dilemma: When we studied '*The Second Exodus*'[173], I shared that when Jesus first returns to earth on Yom Teruah[174], He will come to gather His Elect, His Bride. That includes those who are saved and waiting for His glorious appearing but also for unsaved Israel, to come as their long-awaited Messiah. It is on this return of Jesus as the Lamb (also the Son of Man), that the resurrection of the righteous and rapture will occur and all those who are ready will enter into Heaven with a glorified body just like the Lord's body[175]. But for the redemption of Israel Jesus will remain upon the earth for a short time as the Lamb and He will lead them at first into the wilderness to restore them into the marriage covenant and then back to Mount Zion along the Highway of

---

apostles were all Jewish. But it's not their nationality referenced in Revelation 21:14 but who they were in relation to the Lamb. They represent the atoning work of Jesus to Israel, but as apostles, they also represent the missional reach of the Gospel to all who will receive their Messiah, both Jew and Gentile.

[172] Ezekiel 20:35.
[173] Quick Bites 47 to 55.
[174] Viz the Feast of Trumpets.
[175] Beloved, now we are children of God; and it has not yet been revealed what we shall be, but we know that when He is revealed, we shall be like Him, for we shall see Him as He is. (1 John 3:2 NKJV).

Holiness. However, this creates a real conundrum! Since the rapture will have already taken place by the time the 144.000 return to Mount Zion, how is it these newly redeemed are able to enter into Heaven to join those already there to complete the Bride? As always, I will share my thoughts not as absolute but as my personal belief and best fit from the Bridal lens. Let's head back to Revelation chapter fourteen for a short exposition on the first three verses and see if they can tell us anything more.

Then I looked, and behold, a Lamb standing on Mount Zion, and with Him one hundred and forty-four thousand, having His Father's name written on their foreheads. (Revelation 14:1 NKJV).

First of all, let's look at the symbolism here: The last time we saw the Lamb was in Revelation chapter five where He was hailed as the One worthy to take the scroll and to open its seven seals[176]. On that occasion, the Lamb who symbolises our Lord Jesus Christ was in Heaven but now in Revelation chapter fourteen, He is no longer in Heaven. Jesus has come down to earth and is standing upon Mount Zion. Also symbolic is the number 144,000 which as we have previously seen represents the Bride. Then finally, the Father's name written on their foreheads goes beyond the description of the seal of protection on the forehead found in Revelation 7:3 [177] and

---

[176] But one of the elders said to me, "Do not weep. Behold, the Lion of the tribe of Judah, the Root of David, has prevailed to open the scroll and to loose its seven seals." And I looked, and behold, in the midst of the throne and of the four living creatures, and in the midst of the elders, stood a Lamb as though it had been slain, having seven horns and seven eyes, which are the seven Spirits of God sent out into all the earth. Then He came and took the scroll out of the right hand of Him who sat on the throne. (Revelation 5:5-7 NKJV).

[177] saying, "Do not harm the earth, the sea, or the trees till we have sealed the servants of our God on their foreheads." (Revelation 7:3 NKJV).

symbolises ownership and adoption[178] [179]. But since the context of this whole passage is about the 144,000 following the Lamb wherever He goes, let us not allegorise Mount Zion here as anything other than the promised physical location of the eternal throne where the Lord shall reign upon the earth.[180]

Now despite the obvious symbolism in this passage, we can be assured there is a literal interpretation also. For here we are presented with a glorious glimpse into the returned and redeemed tribes of Israel standing with their Saviour upon Mount Zion all of which are very real. To have arrived here is to have survived the great tribulation[181], to have experienced ten days of awe and wrath against the nations[182] and to have been saved individually and corporately on the Day of Atonement. In an act of great deliverance, the Lord has been in their midst and met with them face to face. He has been

---

[178] Once again, we see this beautiful interplay between adoption and betrothal. For the Son has come to restore us as many children to the Father in a personal and intimate relationship, but the Father presents us corporately to His Son as one Bride.

[179] Incidentally, this mark vividly contrasts with the mark of the beast either on the hand or forehead stamped upon its followers: 'He causes all, both small and great, rich and poor, free and slave, to receive a mark on their right hand or on their foreheads' (Revelation 13:16 NKJV).

[180] I will make the lame a remnant, And the outcast a strong nation; So the LORD will reign over them in Mount Zion From now on, even forever. (Micah 4:7 NKJV).

It will so happen that everyone who calls on the name of the LORD will be delivered. For on Mount Zion and in Jerusalem there will be those who survive, just as the LORD has promised; the remnant will be those whom the LORD will call. (Joel 2:32 NET).

[181] For which the 144,000 were sealed three and a half years earlier

[182] This wrath is not the seven bowls which are yet to be poured out once the Bride is in Heaven but is the wrath of the Lamb (Revelation 6:16,17) who will 'go forth and fight against those nations, as He fights in the day of battle.' (Zechariah 14:3 NKJV).

at their head and led them upon a '*Highway of Holiness*', from the *'wilderness of the peoples'* in Edom, all the way back to Mount Zion in Jerusalem.[183]

And I heard a voice from heaven, like the voice of many waters, and like the voice of loud thunder. And I heard the sound of harpists playing their harps. (Revelation 14:2 NKJV).

The apostle John's focus is now drawn to the mysterious sounds he hears coming from Heaven. The description here is '*a voice from heaven like the voice of many waters*' and '*like the voice of loud thunder*'. Though we find such descriptions elsewhere in the Bible[184], here there is a plurality in their number but a singularity in their voice. John's continuation sheds further light: '*I heard the sound of harpists playing their harps.*'

They sang as it were a new song before the throne, before the four living creatures, and the elders; and no one could learn that song except the hundred and forty-four thousand who were redeemed from the earth. (Revelation 14:3 NKJV).

Remember at this point Heaven's population has just had a huge upgrade[185]. There will be those who, like the five wise virgins, were

---

[183] For an in-depth study about this final pilgrimage of Israel please refer to Quick Bites 47-55.

[184] His feet were like fine brass, as if refined in a furnace, and His voice as the sound of many waters; (Revelation 1:15). See also Ezekiel 1:24, Ezekiel 43:2.

[185] I want to point out how Revelation 14 does present some chronological challenges if we take the way in which John writes to always be sequential. For example, Revelation 14:14-20 contains a duration of time spanning from the rapture and end-time harvest to the Battle of Armageddon and it is within this timeframe that Revelation 14:1-5 occurs. But from a literary perspective, the passage on Mount Zion has to be

ready when Jesus came for them now raptured and transformed into His glorious state. And there will be all those countless souls through the ages already in Heaven who have just received their resurrected bodies. Wow, can you imagine it? What rapturous praise we shall certainly sing together on that day! But there will be more than one new song Heaven will host during that time. For example, we read of a new song in Revelation 5:9,10:

And they sang a new song, saying: "You are worthy to take the scroll, And to open its seals; For You were slain, And have redeemed us to God by Your blood Out of every tribe and tongue and people and nation, And have made us kings and priests to our God; And we shall reign on the earth."[NKJV]

But this is not the same new song that we read of in Revelation 14:3. Why? Because the song in Revelation 5:9 is sung by the saints still upon the earth[186] before the opening of the seven seals and its focus is upon the worthiness of the Lamb to take the scroll and to open its seals. Whereas the new song in Revelation 14:3 will be sung by the saints in heaven after the seals have been opened and seven trumpets

---

written either before or after and in this case John we assume has been instructed to write it down first. Furthermore, when considering the placement of Revelation 14:1-5 we should note that it follows immediately after the mark of the beast passage in Revelation 13:11-18 which includes details of another 'lamb', but which spoke like a dragon. The parallels are significant. Revelation 14:1-5 makes a stark contrast and remedy for Revelation 13:11-18.

[186] The identity of those singing a new song comes directly from the preceding verse:

Now when He had taken the scroll, the four living creatures and the twenty-four elders fell down before the Lamb, each having a harp, and golden bowls full of incense, which are the prayers of the saints. (Revelation 5:8 NKJV).

sounded[187]. In Revelation 5:9 we are given the words that are sung, but not so in Revelation 14:3, this is a song reserved especially for that time and for that company of believers who will collectively incorporate and complete the Bride.

> *There are songs that only the Bride can hear, songs that only she can learn, and songs that only she can sing. I believe this is as true now as it will be then!*

In Revelation 14:3 there is something different being heard in Heaven, a new sound coming like never before. This new song in Heaven will be heard and learnt by those standing with the Lamb upon the earth on Mount Zion. Oh how beautiful, I hope you catch this: for the first time in all of history, there will be an actual harmony between Jew and Gentile that's never been heard before! A convergence will take place on Mount Zion not only of Jew and Gentile but between Heaven and Earth also, where the veil between the visible and invisible realms will be removed, the sky rolled back like a scroll[188] and a touchpoint established between that which is seen and that which is unseen. I cannot explain how this will happen, but I can give you scriptural support.

Then the LORD will create over all of Mount Zion and over those who assemble there a cloud of smoke by day and a glow of flaming fire by night; over all the glory there will be a canopy. (Isaiah 4:5 NIV).

---

[187] The seven bowls of wrath are yet to be released.

[188] And all the powers of the heavens shall melt, and the sky shall be rolled up like a scroll: and all the stars shall fall like leaves from a vine, and as leaves fall from a fig-tree. (Isaiah 34:4 LXX).

Then the sky receded as a scroll when it is rolled up, and every mountain and island was moved out of its place. (Revelation 6:14 NKJV).

We will explore this verse in more detail next time and bring all these wonderful truths together and see how the Lord beautifully fulfils all the Autumn Feasts at the climax of this extraordinary period of the Lamb upon Mount Zion with the 144,000.

QB60 The 144,000 (Part 5)

Here we will not only conclude this mini-series on the 144,000 but also volume one of '*The Gospel According To The Bride*'. Last time, I shared how the need for a rapture immediately after the great tribulation will have changed by the time Jesus returns as the Lamb back to Mount Zion with the 144,000. That's because I believe something supernatural will take place on Mount Zion in those days that will provide a different means of entry into Heaven. Let's pick up the narrative from where we ended last time and look at Isaiah 4:5 again.

Then the LORD will create over all of Mount Zion and over those who assemble there a cloud of smoke by day and a glow of flaming fire by night; over all the glory there will be a canopy. [NIV]

I just love this verse, there's so much here for us to unpack, further study would be well rewarded. How often have you read this verse or heard a sermon on it? How is it we have not seen this before or is it just me getting excited here? This verse sits in a wider prophecy of Isaiah concerning the future of Jerusalem, it hasn't yet been fulfilled because it will be as the Bible so often tells us '*in that Day*'[189] meaning the Day of the Lord. Just as Israel experienced the Divine cloud and fire for forty years in the wilderness until they reached the

---

[189] In that day the Branch of the LORD will be beautiful and glorious, and the fruit of the land will be the pride and glory of the survivors in Israel. (Isaiah 4:2 NIV).

Jordan river[190], so all those who assemble on Mount Zion will experience the cloud and fire of glory again. The glory of God will come down upon this sacred site just as it did on Mount Sinai when Moses met with the Lord face to face. And just as it did in the wilderness during the first exodus, the manifestation of God's presence[191] will descend upon Mount Zion as a lasting touchpoint between Heaven and Earth.

Now for me, here's the real clincher: Isaiah writes *'over all the glory there will be a canopy'*. This word *'canopy'* (Strongs H2646) is where we get the word chuppâh[192] which is the Bridal Canopy under which the ancient Jewish wedding took place. We see this word used two other times in scripture and on both occasions, it describes a bridal chamber[193]. How glorious a picture we are given here of Mount Zion and the returning 144,000. When we look through the Bridal lens what a splendid vision we see, and how wonderfully the Lord has

---

[190] From this point on they were to follow the Ark of the Covenant (Joshua 3:3).

[191] And the LORD went before them by day in a pillar of cloud to lead the way, and by night in a pillar of fire to give them light, so as to go by day and night. (Exodus 13:21 NKJV).
And the Angel of God, who went before the camp of Israel, moved and went behind them; and the pillar of cloud went from before them and stood behind them. (Exodus 14:19 NKJV).

[192] A chuppah (also huppah) is defined as a canopy under which the bride and bridegroom stand during a Jewish wedding ceremony. It symbolises the home the married couple will build together. It is open on all sides to represent the welcome and hospitality that everyone could expect when they entered the tent of Abraham and Sarah.

[193] It is like a bridegroom coming out of his chamber (H2646), like a champion rejoicing to run his course. (Psalms 19:5 NIV).
Gather the people, Sanctify the congregation, Assemble the elders, Gather the children and nursing babes; Let the bridegroom go out from his chamber, And the bride from her dressing room(H2646). (Joel 2:16 NKJV).

interwoven all the prophetic destinies of His Bride together. There will be a chuppâh over Mount Zion! Hallelujah! The glory and presence of God will come down manifested in the cloud and the fire and over it all will be a chuppâh, a bridal canopy!

This is a very different picture to when Jesus first returns as the Son of Man. At that time, Jerusalem will be surrounded by hostile nations and her inhabitants in need of a deliverer[194]. There will have been three and a half years of great tribulation, the darkness of man's iniquity will be at its peak and Mystery Babylon, the *'mother of harlots and abominations of the earth'* [195], will be fully intoxicated[196]. The wedding canopy will not yet be over Mount Zion; not until Israel is redeemed and brought back to Jerusalem will this lasting touchpoint between Heaven and Earth be finally established. Yes, a rapture will be necessary when Jesus first comes, a harvest of the ready and waiting Bride from off the face of the earth, but not so on that glorious return of the 144,000 as they follow the Lamb all the way to Mount Zion. Why? Because when the new song sung in Heaven before the throne is harmonized by the redeemed Bride upon the earth the Wife will have finally made herself ready[197] and Mount Zion will be enshrined by the glory of God.

> *At this point the need for rapture will no longer be necessary because Heaven has come down. Wow, how*

---

[194] Romans 11:26.
[195] Revelation 17:5.
[196] I saw the woman, drunk with the blood of the saints and with the blood of the martyrs of Jesus. And when I saw her, I marvelled with great amazement. (Revelation 17:6 NKJV).
[197] Since from this point the Bride will be in Heaven until the wedding of the Lamb, there are no more 'righteous acts of the saints' (Revelation 19:8) to be fulfilled and therefore the wedding garments are complete.

| *incredible, we really have to just stop and let the mind of Christ illuminate our thinking to a whole new level.*

I realise I'm sharing things you've probably never heard before, but I hope you can see everything I'm presenting here is supported in scripture. Here's what the last verse of the 144,000 standing with the Lamb says will happen on Mount Zion.

And in their mouth was found no guile: for they are without fault before the throne of God. (Revelation 14:5 NKJV).[198]

Did you catch that? It's really easy to miss. In Revelation 14:1 we saw the 144,000 standing on Mount Zion with the Lamb, but now in verse five we read *'they are without fault before the throne of God'*. I believe we should not try to allegorise these two texts but accept them both for how they are written. That these 144,000 who will stand upon Mount Zion in Jerusalem, will also be found blameless before the Throne of God. They are in both the physical and spiritual realms, both in the seen and unseen. I am not saying that the two will happen simultaneously, only that there has been a development in John's vision from seeing them at first in the physical realm and then in the spiritual realm. A transition has taken place. Indeed, in the following chapter Revelation 15 we see this great bridal company now at last all together this time standing on a

---

[198] Not all translations will have the second half of this verse, but only those based on the Textus Receptus, for example the King James Version. Over centuries the Textus Receptus has stood up to scrutiny and remains in my opinion a very reliable text. And so, after prayer, I have felt it right to include Revelation 14:5 in its entirety.

sea of glass mixed with fire and they are singing the song of Moses and the Lamb.[199] [200]

And now I just have one final thought to share with you. After this wonderful journey looking at scripture through the Bridal lens, I can think of no better ending for this first volume than to help us realise when Jesus will one day stand on Mount Zion with the 144,000 it will mark the prophetic fulfilment of the Feast of Tabernacles. This, the last of all the Lord's Feasts, is the one we will take with us into eternity. All of the others will have been fulfilled historically but the Feast of Tabernacles will be perpetual because we will live in the continual manifestation of the Presence of God who will come to reign and tabernacle with man forever. Just like the spring feasts were all fulfilled in quick succession on Jesus' first coming, so will the autumn feasts be on His second. Previously we have studied how the Feast of Trumpets and the Day of Atonement are fulfilled through the return of Jesus when He comes to deliver Israel, but here on Mount Zion is the prophetic completion of all the autumn feasts.

---

[199] And I saw something like a sea of glass mingled with fire, and those who have the victory over the beast, over his image and over his mark and over the number of his name, standing on the sea of glass, having harps of God. They sing the song of Moses, the servant of God, and the song of the Lamb, saying: "Great and marvellous are Your works, Lord God Almighty! Just and true are Your ways, O King of the saints! Who shall not fear You, O Lord, and glorify Your name? For You alone are holy. For all nations shall come and worship before You, For Your judgments have been manifested." (Revelation 15:2-4 NKJV).
[200] Revelation 15 also includes details about the 'seven golden bowls full of the wrath of God' (v7). It is not until the Bride both Jew and Gentile have been safely gathered and in Heaven that the wrath of God through the seven bowls is released.

When Jesus stands on Mount Zion with the 144,000 it will be the fulfilment of the Feast of Tabernacles. Why do I say this? Well, first of all, there are only fifteen days between the Feast of Trumpets and the Feast of Tabernacles, and since Jesus has already been upon the earth with Israel for at least ten days to the Day of Atonement, there are only a few more days for Tabernacles to be fulfilled. Then secondly, the Feast of Tabernacles is a pilgrimage festival, the other two being Passover and Pentecost, when the ancient Israelites were required to return back to the temple in Jerusalem to celebrate the Feast. The difference now is that Jesus Himself will lead Israel on that pilgrimage back to Mount Zion. For the third reason I see this as a prophetic fulfilment of the Feast of Tabernacles let's read from Isaiah 4:5 once more:

Then the LORD will create over all of Mount Zion and over those who assemble there a cloud of smoke by day and a glow of flaming fire by night; over all the glory there will be a canopy.

We have already seen how there will be a covering over Mount Zion, but this verse has one more secret to reveal. For it is not only Mount Zion mentioned here which will be under this bridal canopy, but reference is also made to '*those who assemble there*'. This word '*assemble*' is the word miqrā' (Strongs H4744) and means '*sacred assembly*' or '*convocation*', it is the same word used in Leviticus 23 which describes the Feasts of the Lord in great detail including Tabernacles.

And finally, the fourth reason I believe this picture of the Lamb standing on Mount Zion with the 144,000 is the fulfilment of the Autumn Feasts is because the Feast of Tabernacles is also known as the Feast of Ingathering when all the crops were gathered at the end of the harvest. This is exactly what we have seen in these last two series of '*The Second Exodus*' and '*The 144,000*'. What a perfect picture we have here of this fulfilment. The Feast of Ingathering which Israel has remembered for thousands of years has always been about God's promise to her. After all her dispersion throughout the corners of the earth, Israel will finally be gathered in and come home. The Lord will come for her as He will for us.

Even though there will be a literal fulfilment of this great ingathering and pilgrimage to Mount Zion through the wilderness, there is a way in which we are already on this voyage now. There is a journey for the Bride to take. The way to Mount Zion is through the desert. The way to the Throne Room is upon a Highway of Holiness. O, we do not know how we should venture since we have never been this way before, except the glory of God will go before us in a way which is discernible to those who have ears to hear what the Spirit is saying to the Bride. But more than this, if we look carefully, we will see the footsteps of the Lamb who has gone before us to guide us through the night; for the Lamb who will one day stand on Mount Zion is also our Good Shepherd who has come to lead us safely home.

Epilogue

Wow, what an awesome finale! I can only share these things from a personal conviction and not as an absolute, but even if you do not agree with me, I hope you will at least be gracious enough to accept how I have endeavoured to honour the Biblical narrative and hold to scripture whilst on a personal journey of learning and intimacy with my Bridegroom King. This first volume of '*The Gospel According to the Bride*' has been such a privilege to write and is a window into my own study life and intimacy with Jesus. If you have reached this far, I thank you for taking the time to join me on this journey, and my prayer is that more than my words, you will have heard His Words in your spirit romancing you with a greater vision and understanding of just how much He loves you and has prepared a glorious future for all those who will heed the call to prepare for His return. There is so much more I have to share and so I am already planning volume two of '*The Gospel According to the Bride*' which I will release in this Quick Bite format. And so how do I bring these sixty Quick Bites to an end? Well, I would like to do so in two ways: First, to encourage you to make the same heart's response that Rebekkah made when asked if she would go to the Bridegroom. For the Holy Spirit has come to lead us to Jesus, this time not as our Saviour but as our Bridegroom. Therefore, when asked if we will go with the Holy Spirit on this new quest, let us with eagerness of heart respond "I will go", and secondly after all is said and done there is only one prayer that is fitting, one call that remains, let us pray therefore the prayer that only the Bride can pray and join with the Spirit in saying

"Amen, Even So, Come Lord Jesus".

Now to Him who is able to keep you from stumbling, And to present you faultless Before the presence of His glory with exceeding joy, -

To God our Saviour, Who alone is wise, Be glory and majesty, Dominion and power, Both now and forever. Amen. –

(Jude 1:24, 25 NKJV)

About the Author

Mike Pike was called to be a missionary at age ten and has spent his life on the mission field in the UK and in many other countries around the world. He carries a prophetic mantle to align nations to their Bridal destiny and teaches an outpouring of the Holy Spirit reserved only for the Bride to help her get dressed. His vision is for the Bride around the world to gather in times of repentance and worship and cry 'Amen, Even So, Come Lord Jesus'. He oversees the Call2Come movement together with Howard Barnes. He is married to Jo and together they have raised five children and now live in Cornwall, England.

About Call2Come

Call2Come is a growing movement around the world primarily focussed on the Second Coming of Jesus Christ and the implications of this 'blessed hope' for the church today. Our mandate is to help the Bride get ready. This preparation is both inward and individual for each believer to grow in their love and intimacy with Jesus Christ, but also outward and corporate.

Our vision: In regions and nations around the world, the Bride of Christ will gather together in times of worship and prayer, to pour out her heart in purity of longing, repentance and proclamation, and ask Jesus to Come.

What We Believe:

1. The Bride of Christ has an urgent mandate that only she can fulfil: to make a way for her Bridegroom King, by preparing a highway of holiness for His return, straight paths of righteousness upon which the King of Kings will return.

2. The Bride of Christ must fulfil her mandate and calling before the great day of the Lord. There is work that only she can do, and prayers that only she can pray.

3. The Bride of Christ is a warrior bride! She stands in the nations of the world as a royal princess and wields in her hand the sceptre of the King. She is His glory upon the earth and is so breathtakingly beautiful she has many enemies, intent on her demise. But she is not weak, she is very strong. For she is in Christ, and the corporate expression of oneness in the church.

4. The Bride of Christ is planted in the land to effect national transformation and healing. She is an intercessor, the One 'called by His Name' to pray for the healing of nations. 2 Chronicles 7:14.

5. The Bride of Christ has each anointing of the five-fold office. She is an apostle, a prophet, an evangelist, a pastor and a teacher, because she is just like Jesus who was all of these and more, and therefore the Bride is the perfectly complete and compatible 'wife of the Lamb'.

6. We believe there is an outpouring of the Holy Spirit that the church has not yet experienced, in fact it is one that is reserved only for the Bride. It will not be released by asking for another outpouring or revival but is sent by the Bridegroom King in advance of His coming, to help the Bride of Christ get ready when she begins to call upon Him to come.

Find Out More:

If you've enjoyed 'The Gospel According to the Bride' and would like to find out more, then there are a lot of resources available for further study and encouragement and also a large online community to connect with.

www.call2come.org

www.youtube.com/c/call2come

www.facebook.com/groups/call2come

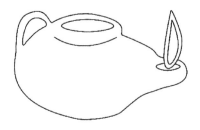

The Spirit and
the Bride say Come

Revelation 22:17 [ESV]